Before the Wax Hardened

Adrian Kenny

Odell & Adair

To Mary and Eva

'. . . Remember the time
Before the wax hardened,
When each of us was like a seal.
Each of us carries the imprint
of the friend met along the way;
In each the trace of each.
For good or evil,
In wisdom or in folly
Each stamped by each . . . .'

From the *The Mirror Maker*
by Primo Levi

A Paperback Original
First Published 1991 by
Odell & Adair

ISBN 1 870489 03 9

This book is published with the financial assistance of **The Arts Council/An Chomhairle Ealaíon, Ireland.**

Cover Design by Pomphrey Associates,
Typeset by Janekoprint.
Printed by the Guernsey Press Ltd.,
Vale, Guernsey, Channel Islands.

I

JOHN EDWARD

Going somewhere, driving from an unfamiliar direction, preoccupied too, it was some time before I realised I was in familiar country. Purple clematis on a white washed farmhouse . . . the sudden dark of a high hedged road: I had my bearings when I came out onto the motorway. There was the pub, teak-windowed now, on a raised beach of loose chippings. On the other side—the signpost pointing up the squat steep hill. Joining the traffic, accelerating again, I glanced in the rear view mirror and saw myself ascend it twenty years before.

******

The headmaster led the way down a wide, high-windowed corridor—'I've always found the better a fellow has been brought up, the less fuss he makes about his quarters.'

I smiled back and he opened a door into some narrower, darker passage. He stumbled against a fire extinguisher, then opened another door and stood politely aside. An iron school bed, a plywood chair and wardrobe and a mat of jackdaws' twigs on the hearth.

'Really . . . these girls.' He gathered up the twigs and set them in the grate, spanked pink hands off one another. 'No fires, if it's all the same to you.' He patted a radiator, then fiddled with the stopcock.

When I had unpacked, I went for a walk down the avenue, then down the road. A line of cars was coming up, bringing the boys back to school. Registration numbers from all over Ireland.

Tow-bars. My stomach seized up with misery.

At the bottom of the hill was the main road, being widened into a motorway. Dublin 60—the signpost was lying against a broken ditch. A break in the eastward traffic and I was on the cats' eyes; a break in the westward line and I was across the road and into a pub I had often noticed when I was one of those travellers.

'And now the Mullingar millionaire, Joe Dolan! "I'm on an Island and I've Got No Place Left to Run." Take it away, Joe!'

A man behind the counter turned down the radio, looked up from a newspaper and read me slowly from head to shoes. 'Not a bad old day.'

'Nice old pub.'

'Old is right.' He watched me play a solitary game of darts between sips of beer. 'On the holidays?'

'Not exactly.' I threw a few more darts before I owned up. I was going to teach junior English, French, Latin and Nature Study in the school up the road.

He took my glass and topped it up foaming. I said 'Whoah' and in a minute we were into the G.A.A., horses, Northern Ireland and the latest Cortina. I felt my armpits slobber with perspiration as I mistook Gowran Park for a football team. I tried to save face, taking a quarter pint in one gulp but he had returned to his newspaper as I looked back from the door.

It had all taken about three minutes. Joe Dolan was singing the same song. I sang it to myself as I walked back up the hill. Lying in my iron bed that night, I heard it on the transistor my father had given me. It was in the air all that autumn of 1968. Down in the rushy rugby field the boys sang it in the scrum and on the long Sunday afternoon crocodile walks too, until I knew it by heart. I used to hum it to myself as I wondered how I had ended up here: my first pause for thought; a small crossroads

4

like the one at the bottom of the hill. Even in Prep, as they called evening study, I hummed it, leaning against the rail before the glowing Romesse stove, looking at the rows of bent heads, going over the past in my own head. Do we weave an image of the past deliberately as a magpie roofs its nest? Or spend our life pulling away at that impenetrable first roof?

1

Spring. Morning, 1955. Mythic details.

Around the breakfast table: father, mother and growing children—my family, clear as the vista of hills from the Rathmines Road that vanishes as you approach below blue rooftops.

74 ... 76 ... The same postman had served the house for years and still no one knew even his Christian name ... 78.

'Post!'

'Ssh!'

'After the time signal—'

'Ssh! Ssh!'

'It's only the *Tribune* '—

"Oh, my God!' My father got to his feet and stood under the wireless. Silence! for the voice from that high shelf which on other mornings announced the climbing of Everest, the death of Stalin ... all those items we heard out patiently before—

'And the weather .... '

The announcer drew breath and my mother said as one quick quiet word 'Maybe in God it'd rain and you'd sell some wellingtons.'

'... Rain spreading from the West.'

She breathed out a silent aspiration and cut open the twine of the parcelled up *Connaught Tribune* and out fell—

'A letter!'

She glanced at us, then around at the open kitchen door, miming a Ssh! of her own.

'Will ye have more tea?' Sure enough, in stepped Delia, eyes country-quick as Mama's, hoovering up newspaper, envelope and letter.

'. . . and a request now for the O'Reilly family in Edenderry. That's Josie, Ron, Brid-Nuala, Angela . . . . '

'Are you right?' My father emptied his cup and stood up.

In ten minutes the house was empty except for my mother and Delia, and the letter. I pictured it glowing pink behind the Sacred Heart lamp—our letter-holder, scalding Delia with curiosity as they went about the washing, bed-making and cooking, always together; my mother giving out carefully selected morsels.

'Delia, you didn't know any Rodgers in Spaddagh?'

'Sure I know Spaddagh well. Don't you know—'

'They say he killed himself.'

'What are you saying, Mrs Kenny?'

'They got the gun beside him on the table and a string on the trigger tied to the latch of the door. They say he must have called the dog in out of the street.'

'Oh my God, Mrs Kenny!'

'And did you know him?'

'Didn't I know him well! Don't you know—'

'They shot the dog.' Mama let the talk fall back to the subject. All day long backing and advancing, never quite meeting, went their conversation. They came from the same part of the country. Mama wore an apron like Delia's and was sometimes mistaken for the 'maid', a word I used once in their company. They had been sitting together at the fire, darning socks, and had both lowered their heads in embarrassed silence.

Down the mid-morning empty road came the cavalcade of carts and vans: milk man, bread man, waste man, egg man . . . and then the messenger boys. Together my mother and Delia dealt with them, together again they darned and answered the door to the mid-afternoon procession of beggars, tinkers and charity collectors who had discovered this house. Together with the family after tea, Delia would join in the Rosary below the

Sacred Heart lamp, where the letter still glowed.

But no rain. Out came a hot April sun instead. My father seemed in no hurry this morning and as we drove to school, he went by a new, longer way, turning down a wide road with chestnut trees on either side. A maid in uniform letting up a blind looked out as we stopped. The V8 engine began its hysterical turning-over. My father rolled down his window and pointed to a *For Sale* sign, with *Sold* nailed over, standing in a garden. The roof and bay windows seemed huge.

'That's your new house, boys.' He gave the engine a rev. 'Didn't you know that boy Murphy in school?'

'He's gone to Canada.'

'That's the one. That's where he used to live.' Rolling up the window again and answering our questions, he drove on to school.

I had sat beside William in school: a big quiet boy with orange hair and wide ears. He had not come back after the Christmas holidays and, when his desk was taken away, we were told he had gone to Canada. We were not told why, but 'To have his ears cut off' appeared from nowhere, as mysterious and convincing as a catechism answer.

Up the avenue went the line of cars: Rovers, Humbers, some shining black ones with C.D. on the back—which I thought stood for Canada—and a few small ones. The big ones, driven by men, dropped off boys in maroon blazers on the gravel island and turned and drove away again. The small ones, from each rolled-down window a woman's head jutted out, stayed behind making a corral around the rector.

'Great Scott!' He laughed, lifted his biretta, scratched his head and, replacing the biretta, strolled to the next window.

'Father O'Conor is a gentleman,' my mother said. The very way he walked up the big steps of the schoolhouse made it seem as small as our own. He stood under the fanlight looking at his pocket watch and from the other house the priests appeared one by one, chatting under a matching peacock tail of glass for a moment, then coming down the steps, each carrying a little pyramid of exercise books, books, chalk box and duster. Father O'Conor's own house in the west of Ireland was as big as both these houses put together, my father said. He leaned out of the window to tighten my tie, spannering up the knot with a finger and thumb until it was as hard as a nut, and then following the procession down the avenue.

The first time I had come here I thought we had taken a short cut into the country. Turning off the busy main road through a gap between houses, we went up an avenue between bushy back garden walls, past a lodge and then between a field of snoring cattle and another where a man in a white polo neck was mowing with the scythe. Now the same man, in a black gown and with a roman collar as high as the polo neck, was blowing a whistle. We all formed up in lines.

'In the name—'
Pause, as a desk seat rattled. Silence.
'—of the Father and the Son and of the Holy Ghost. Amen. Hail Mary full of grace the Lord . . . .'
Pause, and our lazy voice was shown up. Father O'Conor's eyes ran over us from mouth to mouth, his own moving again as our voice rose. Pause again as we rose too loud, moving with us again . 'Now and at the hour of our death. Amen.'
'Father, may I leave the room?'
'Quickly.' Father O'Conor thought of something. 'And, Owen—'
'Yes, Father?'
'Turn on the taps a moment, please.'

Lucky Owen. We listened to the water while Father O'Conor stood in a corner and leaned an ear to a pipe going up a wall. Everything in the room was new except his gown. He took a bit of bright brass pipe screw from his pocket and looked through it at the light, then left it on the table beside his breviary and *Latin For Today*.

'Will I tell him, Father?'

'Father, look what someone did to the floor.'

Someone pointed to a scrape on the new tiles right beside my desk.

'Adrian?'

'It was William, Father.'

'Is it true, Father, about William?'

'Yes, they've gone to Canada.'

'To have his ears cut off?'

'By Jove!' Father O'Conor laughed, his eyes running across the rest of the floor and along the new painted walls and the rows of yellow varnished desks.

'We've bought his house, Father.'

'Father, how old is this house?'

Father O'Conor took up his grammar, but slowly. 'I should think about a hundred and twenty years.'

'And how old are you, Father?'

'Father, couldn't you be King of Ireland, if you wanted to? That's what my father said—'

But Father O'Conor had stopped smiling and, as if a skin had been peeled from his face, he wore now a chilling expression. 'Good grief.'

A mouse!

It ran across the bright floor and into the library, a cupboard in the wall. We got up to watch Father O'Conor go down on one knee and open the door. His hand, drawing from under a frayed black sleeve a frayed white cuff held by pale gold oval links, reached to part the rows of books: *The House at Pooh Corner, The Bog of Stars, The Children of the New Forest* ....

'Father!'

In fright the mouse jumped down onto the floor again, down the avenue of shining shoes, skating like a dodgem car by the skirting board, all the way around and back into the library again. Father O'Conor shut the door. The cold look left his face, but no one spoke.

'Now. Open your books, please. Without bending them back. Now—' He put a hand in his pocket—another clink of metal—and took out a crumb of chalk. 'Now. What did I do just then, when I opened the door? I went down on one knee ... I. . . ?'

'Knelt, Father?'

'When we go into chapel first we—?'

'Genuflect!'

'We genuflect. we "flect" the "genu". Now ....' He caught the crumb in his nails and wrote the two words on the blackboard. 'Now. What do we do when we genuflect?'

'We flect the genu, Father.'

'In English, we—?'

'Genuflect.'

'But how do we genuflect? We bend our—?'

'Leg, Father?'

'No.'

'Foot.'

'No.'

'Knee.'

'Thank you, Adrian. We bend our knee. We flect our ... ?

'Genu.'

'Good. So genu means—?'

'Knee.'

'And flect means—?'

'Bend.'

'Flect means bend. Now . . . .' Father O'Conor looked out of the window. 'Now. Can anyone tell me another word we get from flect? Flect—flex—flexi . . . .'

Two dozen pairs of eyes followed the long white hand opening and closing in the air.

'Flexible.' Again Father O'Conor took up *Latin For Today*, put it down again.'Now—'

There was a knock at the door and we all stood up. We all sat down again. Father Williams flicked his pencil down the roll-book, as easily as he swung the scythe.

'Peter, Father.'

'Mmm . . . .' He shut the roll-book, opened another. 'Milk?' He counted hands with the pencil point. 'Two bottles?' He counted again. 'Gentlemen.'

We stood up and sat down again.

'Flexible . . . .' Father O'Conor looked out of the window again and then, as briskly as Father Williams, he suddenly dusted the chair with a wing of his gown and sat down, his book held up straight before him.

'"Vasto"—and the stress is on the first syllable. "Vas-to. Vas—"?'

'—to.'

'We'll begin.'

But by my Hopalong Cassidy watch, class was over.

The next class was different. Father Wilmot came in and said the Hail Mary and the right hand that gestured Amen to his breast continued smoothly to the table for his books. He never sat at the rostrum but came down into the class, sitting on one of our desks and moving the owner to sit in with another boy. He gestured to a window and a boy shut it a little. Already Father O'Conor was outside, steadying his biretta with one hand as he made his way across the fields. Another gesture, lordly as Father O'Conor's—yet different somehow, and another boy wiped the board clean of 'flect' and 'genu'. Silence then for a whole minute while he polished his glasses with a snow white handkerchief.

Then—

'Well, who was listening to the "The Foley Family" last night?'

Someone put his hand up and snapped fingers. Father Wilmot looked politely past him as if he had farted.

'We don't listen to Radio Eireann . . . .' Rory sounded sure of the right answer, but he too went red as Father Wilmot glanced past him.

'Jim?'

'Yes, Father?'

'Wasn't it very good? "Sufferin' duck—"' Father Wilmot said with a Dublin accent. I was ready to supply more, but Father Wilmot had moved on and was telling us now about a meeting he had been to the previous night where an—he paused and nodded slowly—ordinary working man had stood up from the audience and made his point with—he nodded slowly again—absolute clarity. Somehow this reminded him of something else. Now he was telling us about a place called Emo, his noviciate, and about a boy who had worked in the kitchen there who, when he had blacked and polished the range, would say—Father Wilmot imitated a country accent, though not so well as a Dublin one—'There's style in that.'

In his own voice he said 'What's style?'

'Father.'

'Jim?'

'Jack Kyle has style.'

'Good. And Anthony?'

A few minutes of this and then, smoothly as if we had reached the end of a page, Father Wilmot turned to the book open on his knees, stroking it flat with the backs of his fingers. He gave a small yawn and said 'Tell me, did I give you memory work?'

While someone recited, he took off his wrist watch and left it on the desk beside him. Later in the class he might take off his glasses and leave them on another desk. Our exercise books were gathered on a third and so on until he occupied the whole front of the class. He spoke so low that the boys at the back had to lean forward to hear. When the bell rang, he paused irritably as if an aeroplane was flying over and then continued, often for five minutes beyond the time.

This must have annoyed Father Rowan, for the first part of our break was taken up by his Rosary. As we ran outside, Father Williams called 'Walk, gentlemen!' As we walked we saw Father Rowan standing in the courtyard and we ran again. Father Rowan's shoes were patched and, when he flected his genu, we saw that his socks were lumpy with darns, but he too had a manner as commanding as Father O'Conor or Father Wilmot. There was something thrilling about the way, the morning he saw a boy talking during prayers, his face hardened red like a woman's and he walked up to the boy and slapped him across the cheek.

There as we prayed was Father O'Conor outside again, discussing something with the gardener's wife, who stood in her cottage door with a dripping mop in one hand and a red-haired baby in the other. In his hand, Father O'Conor had a broken budding branch and as we ran outside into the yard he stopped suspects, gently putting out his hand and then firmly clutching them by the elbow and showing them the branch.

'Do you know anything about this?'

'What's that, Father?'

'This is lilac!' His voice grew angrier each time he said it. From someone he must have an explanation. By the end of break, there was a note on the board in his thick-nibbed black writing: *Boys must not play with their balls on the avenue. Chas. O'Conor S.J.*

Ten minutes break and a three-acre field before us.

'Chariots!'

Big boys paired off and bound together and a small boy climbed on their shoulders and was carried full speed down the field, knocking off other charioteers as he went.

'Yip yip alloi! Ben Hur!'

My horses were brothers, Joss and Art, galloping as one and, as the whistle blew, cantering off the end of the field and out of sight down the back avenue. We rounded a bend, passed two senior horses on their hind legs smoking a cigarette, trotted down a path walled by shrubbery and topped with the boles of beech trees. High up were the scars of copperplate initials—A.B. 1891—which, I thought, must once have been as low down as the furtive new ones—A.K.1954—still a terrible yellow in spite of all the clay I had rubbed in.

'Did you really buy Murphy's house?'

'Yep.'

'Then you'll be right beside us.'

Through a flash of bluebells, past a summer house, along an ivied wall, pulling up at the only break in the boundary—a narrow gate set in a fence of high green galvanise whose top was cut into jagged spikes. Outside, the world was going on as usual. A motor car, a guard on his bike, a girl passed by. A bread van halted and the horse put his head into a bag of oats. Joss and Art stepped a foot outside and pawed the pavement with their heels.

'You're meant to be gentlemen in there!' The bread man jumped to catch the bridle as the horse reared and scattered oats high in the air. We wheeled back and galloped the rest of the boundary, whinnying behind the last tree, where I dismounted.

16

When we were inside Father O'Conor was out. Now our class was outside he was in, standing at one of the big front windows looking out over the cricket field. Signor Agnelli felt the gaze bore into his back as he drilled us. He wheeled the column so he was facing the windows. We were behaving well. Two dozen pairs of white canvas shoes marking time in the grass, under each arm a short wooden baton exactly horizontal. Still marking time, Signor Agnelli came down the line calling instructions through the whistle in his mouth; quick-stepped backwards to the head again.

'Attention!'

'Every second boy—' He waved his rhino whip and the line became two lines.

'Close up!'

'Quick march!'

'Sapristi!' He came alongside blowing his whistle. 'Halt!'

We began again and this time both lines were parallel. Straight down the field—a hundred yards, two hundred . . . . Whistle! and the lines peeled apart, marching like duellists in opposite directions. Another shrill and we turned back, marching parallel again, past Father O'Conor's gaze, back to where Signor Agnelli stood, hands on hips, smiling.

'Every week. You mus' be absolutely per-fect!'

'Signor, why?'

'Father O'Conor—he knows.' He glided down on one knee, as he had the day the bishop called, and tied his natty shoe's lace, glancing back at the big window.

We had him again for drawing, the last class of the day. The sun had gone around and left our basement room behind, but Signor Agnelli was making another on the blackboard. With a wooden compass he made a circle three feet high and then on a shorter compass he filled it with petal shapes, as symmetrical as his army drill figures, which he talked about as he worked in the

coloured chalks with the heel of his small olive hand. Yellow .
. . yellow and blue . . . green . . . green and blue . . . yellow.

'And the sergeant, when he got those boys with the white
hands, by jeengo! did he give them work. Kitchens . . . latrines
. . . everything!' Now he was telling us about his days in
Mussolini's army.

Up on tip-toe, fingertipping in white on yellow, he was
reminded of an old Roman academy painter whose studio he
used to visit.

'. . . And when he took the leetle brush and touch the face,
the face of the infant Jesus . . . such ex-pression. My God! Incredible!'

Down on one knee again, smudging blue on red, and now
he was talking about a woman he knew, an opera singer. She had
once used a dressing-room that had been used the night before
by Paul Robeson.

'. . . And the smell. The *smell*. In-de-scribable.'

He cleaned his brilliant hands on his M.A. sleeves and
walked to the back of the class to look at the figure. It was like
a burning wheel. We were even quieter than we were in Father
Wilmot's class. I loved this last class of the day in the way I loved,
after my bath on Saturday night, sitting in front of our kitchen
fire. When we did get up, we stood around Signor while he
nicked out mistakes with a corner of his duster. He skipped into
the air and left the duster out of reach on top of the board. But
next morning Father Hillery, though an inch shorter, had got it
and wiped everything away with a cute grin.

'How are you getting home?'
'Walking.'
'We'll be with you,' Art said. His brother said 'Is Mummy
not calling?'
We went out the back gate but the road was empty, except

for the sparrows still hopping about the horse's spilt oats. Joss and Art never seemed to know if they were being called for or not. My brother and I often passed their mother, sitting in her small car dressed in clothes as bright as Signor Agnelli's drawings. One day she had a high hat like a witch's, but with green veils falling from the crown. Another day she gave us a lift and I noticed she had bandages on her hands. When I asked her why, she said nothing. Not a rude silence, just the way when one day we gave Joss and Art a lift and Joss said 'This is a gas old bus— how old is she?'—my father had said nothing.

A senior boy walked up the footbridge over the railway with us. He told us that Father Wilmot had told them that the most difficult word in the world was the word 'being'. Then he got on his bike and free-wheeled down the other side.

Joss said 'Let's have a look at Murphy's house.'

'Do you know the way?'

'Do you not?' They were amazed. We didn't. My brother and I knew only the bus way home. A single turn off that and we were in the road we had seen that morning, still as empty and quiet; nobody and nothing but the chestnut trees coming into leaf. There was the house. The front garden was full of holes where bushes had been dug up. Joss put his hands through the bars of a side gate and pulled back a bolt and we went down a cement path into a back garden: more big holes in the ground. Everything was gone except the apple trees. There were about a dozen of them, and beyond the wall a dozen more and so on up to the windows of a house as big and old as our school house, so we seemed to be in an orchard—which, we found out later, was what it all had once been.

'Why not? Now it's your house', Art said and, when my brother shrugged, I was bunted up to an open fly window and shoved through like the *Connaught Tribune* that morning. standing on my hands on a window ledge, I looked at them

19

upside down.

'Somersault. Like Signor.'

'Sapristi!'

I fell onto the floorboards. The first thing I noticed was the smell: not nice, though not bad either—like ripe sawn wood.

'Swein hund! Open up.'

'Achtung!'

'Snell! Snell!'

I opened the conservatory door and we ran through the house, counting the rooms, lying in the big bath, and reading the old newspapers that lined the the floors until the sky went dark. The morning forecast was coming true. Mama's prayers had been heard again. Beyond Rathmines church dome and town hall clock tower, framed in one of the front bedroom windows, flat and black as a negative now, were my father's shops packed with people dying for wellingtons. Thank God. There were houses everywhere, except for a space just across the road where a few fields had been spared, like a ringfort in ploughland. A small old nun followed by a sheepdog followed a cow along by a hedge. From beyond the hedge a bell rang and they all went a little faster. We looked at our watches; five to four. When Rathmines clock struck four we left, by the hall door. We delayed again at Joss and Art's house—no one seemed to be in and now they had to get in by the side door—so it was wet evening when we finally got home.

Finding our house empty would have been like finding the Sacred Heart lamp unplugged. There they were, just like the letter above, as we had left them in the morning. Yet my mother had been out, to the fields at the end of our back garden. She had got some rushes there and was trying to make a rattle for my youngest brother. Her memory had taken her three-quarters of the way. She had plaited the handle and half of the top so it was like a hood, but she could not close it over.

'Delia—'

'What's that, Mrs Kenny?' As usual when it was heavy rain, Delia came around to the fire by the long way, away from the window. Once she had been standing under the kitchen fanlight when a freak flash of lightning scorched a mark down the parting of her hair.

'There's some little trick to that and I remember it as well, only—'

'Well, I never saw that done.' Delia took the rattle and stretched her bracked shins to the fire.

'Oh, I have it! Give it to me here till I see.'

'Well, I could no more do that, Mrs Kenny'—Delia turned to us. 'Well, and what did ye learn at school? Was the master cross, tell us?'

There was so much to tell: the King of Ireland—a mouse— a house a hundred and twenty years old. But my brother was telling what Father Hillery had said about Errol Flynn.

'Ear-roll Flynn. He has no fear of the Lord—'

'This is the Eyetalian?'

'No. That's Signor.'

'God, what's he like at all? Has he the oily skin?'

'They do get that from what they eat' Mama said.

'Well, I was at the dance the other night, Mrs Kenny . . . .'

'Where?'

'The Metropole. And if this black lad didn't come up to me. I never saw him with the dark till he was one side of me. Well, I nearly went through the floor.'

'And where was Jack?'

'Sure, he'd gone to get me a mineral.'

'And was he really black?' Mama said. 'He wasn't one of them brown fellows?'

'He was as black as that coal!'

'Had he the shiny teeth?' Mama showed her own teeth,

slightly yellow like the best teeth, and then bent to nip off the end of a rush. 'Run out in the garden and get me a few little stones like a good lad.'

'It's raining—'

'May it never stop. But tell me this and tell me no more,' Delia said. 'The Eyetalian—can he speak English?'

'Now look!' Mama dropped in the wet pebbles, wove over the last little space and turned the loose ends out of sight. 'Haven't I the great memory. Oh, how long is it since my mother made me one of those!'

She gave it to my youngest brother on the floor, and went to ring our father. She rang him every evening before he left work, so if business was bad she knew about it before he came home.

'D-S-I...L-S-N....' The shop code they used sounded like Italian. As usual it meant nothing good. She came back and got my young brother with the rattle ready for bed.

'And me sitting down!' Delia said. As the phone rang, she sat down again. Her ear swung to the door like a compass needle.

'... Yes, Guard .... Thank you, Guard .... I will, Guard.'

I knew at once. Mama came in. We had heard so she had to tell us. Some young roughs had been seen breaking into our new house. The woman next door gave their descriptions to the Guards.

Delia's face looked anxious first, then delighted. 'God—if the boss heard that!'

The letter flap rattled and the *Evening Mail* fell into the hall. In a few minutes, our father would follow. Delia built up the fire. The wireless was turned on, ready for the news and another weather forecast. We heard the key in the lock.

'Not a word about that now—' Mama murmured, as the door slammed shut.

The fields at the back of the house were not neat ones with nuns. From our bedroom window we saw flames of tinkers' fires shooting up beyond the back garden wall. One day I was sitting on the wall when one of their goats jumped up beside me. He jumped after me into the garden and up the path and when I backed against the kitchen door—locked! he lowered his oblong yellow eyes and pressed me with his horns.

I had the same feeling now each time the door downstairs opened. Beyond the fires again were the flat orange glares of the street lamps that fenced a new corporation housing estate. They stood in a line along a high wall topped with barbed wire, but nothing could keep out those other young roughs from the field where we played. One day they caught my brother and tied him to a tree, cut off his hair and burned it at his feet. Every day we saw the Guard, who cycled our road, stopping those gulliers with silver snot stripes on their sleeves. Now, like P.C.49, he was probably pedalling slowly towards our door.

The kitchen door opened.

'I might as well lock up and throw the bloody keys in the Liffey!'

The door slammed and our father's footsteps came up the stairs. My brother hid his face in *The Eagle*. I took my new book from the locker.

'Rosamund ran into the rectory schoolroom and closed the door behind her with the air of someone who has news to tell.

"Have you ever heard of Leonard Stone?" she demanded.

Letty and Tom looked expectant, but David did not even raise his eyes from his book.

"What is the use of asking questions when you know the answers already?" he said and went on reading. David was the only one of the rectory children who could quash Rosamund and even he admitted that it took a lot of pressure. This time she ignored him altogether.

23

"If you know who he is, it may interest you to know that he is coming to live with us," she said. "He is coming next week and—"

"But I don't know who he is," said Helen. She was the youngest of the family and had been promoted to schoolroom life a year ago.

Rosamund looked happier. "Leonard Stone is Daddy's cousin's little boy, and he is coming to live here because his father is to be Colonial Secretary in India—"

"India isn't a colony," interposed David.

"Well something secretary in India! His mother is a tiresome woman, who thinks of nothing but Bridge and dancing and Leonard has been left far too much with the servants, and so . . . . "

I began my first novel.

Next door I heard the big double bed creak. There was a long sigh, and then silence.

2.

'Tell them all I was asking for them!' Delia called from the hall door.

'Don't mind her.' My mother bent to straighten my tie.

'Are you right?' The engine stopped its hysterical turning over and we backed out onto the road. This morning in the back seat there were suitcases instead of schoolbags. We stopped at the KCR and collected *The Eagle*. We had it half read when we stopped again outside a house in Merrion Square.

'The Mekon!'

A small man in gold-buttoned green livery answered the door. An old woman in an astrakhan coat was right behind him, ready to go. The Mekon followed her carrying her bags. She said 'Musha' when she stumbled, but once she was in the front seat she had an amazing grand accent. A young woman, who looked just like her, said 'Goodbye, mother' in an even grander voice, and a tall hairy man in a short-sleeved dentist's coat shouted 'Goodbye, granny!' in the grandest voice of all.

We went West every year, but this year, because of the house-moving, we were being sent earlier. School had just ended. Mrs Hayden told us as soon as we were in the train that she had been a school teacher. I looked out the window: there was the one-armed stationmaster putting a rosebud in his buttonhole, just like last year. Mrs Hayden called me to attention. 'She's grand, only she's one leg in the air,' I had heard my father say, so while I listened I looked at her legs. The one-armed man blew his whistle, the train jumped forward and Mrs Hayden's two legs flew in the air. Soon we were flying along by the canal, counting the herons, while Mrs Hayden explained everything. 'Kill Lucain. Killucan. The church of Lucan. That's the spire. Do you see it? *Cill* is the Irish for church. Are you both good at Irish?'

The train pulled out again and gathered speed and my brother said '*Eaglais*—that's what we say at school.'

'*Eaglais*.' She gave the word a sharp long sound. 'And that's right. That's the more up-to-date word. *Cill* is the old old word, you see. Then there's *Séipéal*.' She smiled at us. 'Have you ever heard of that word. That's an older word than *Eaglais*. It's in the middle. There are lots of words for church in Irish. *Teampall* is the word for a Protestant church. And then there's another word—*Ard Eaglais*. That means—what do you think that means? *Ard Eaglais*?'

'High Church?'

'A high church. A cathedral. We're coming to one now. In Mullingar. I can see it from here already. I remember it being built. Well.'

By the time we reached Athlone I was as tired as if I had walked.

Mrs Hayden was only getting into her stride. '*Ath Luain*. Luan's ford.' She was quiet for a moment as she looked down at the powerful river.

'Like Longford,' I said, like a fool.

'No no no—'

We swung right, up the bare west shore of Lough Ree. She pointed back across the lake. '—No, that's *an Longh Phort* . . . .'

On the left, through the other window, I could see a train steaming out for Galway. I followed its track in the map framed above Mrs Hayden's head . . . turning right at Athenry, then Monivea . . . Tuam . . . up to the dent in the Mayo border where my mother and Delia and every week the *Connaught Tribune* came from. And now Delia was leaving—to get married to the milkman. I had gone with her one evening to see her new home. It was somewhere in town, one big old room with a ceiling as high as our house, our old house, divided in two by a red curtain.

The milkman had stayed on the other side of the curtain.

'Knockcroghery. *Cnoc na Crocaire.* What would you say that means?'

When she told us the history of that, there was the delph factory and that took us most of the way to Castlerea.

'We won't feel now,' she said. 'Now, who do you think lives in there.' She pointed to a thousand flying trees. 'That's a hard one.'

'Who?'

'I'll give you one clue. The King of Ireland.'

'Father O'Conor.'

'How did you know that?'

'We know him.'

I glimpsed the far-off flash of windows. Maybe he was there now, looking out at our train as he wrote my school report, ending as usual 'a trifle giddy'.

We reached Ballinlough without history or etymology. Mrs Hayden was too busy asking us questions about Father O'Conor and yawning casually at our replies and then casually summing up. 'He could have had all that, but no. No, he gave it all up to be a poor ordinary humble priest.'

'He's a Jesuit,' my brother said.

'It makes no difference!' Mrs Hayden said, but her eyes had the same look as Signor Agnelli's when we stood on the rostrum and looked down at him. Nine years old, but I understood— sure as Napoleon.

She looked out the window. 'Loch O'Flynn. We're nearly there.'

'Loch O'Flynn,' my brother murmured. 'The Lake of the Flynns.'

Sure enough, her ears shone red against her astrakhan collar.

' Mrs Hayden—' My brother's eye caught mine and we

began yawning like her, then whimpering to hide our squeals.

'I hope I won't have to speak to your aunt Margaret about you.' But still she kept her face to the green blur out of the window. The train shuddered and the blur went grey and then we stopped outside a giant black-and-white sign.

'Sorry, Mrs Hayden—Béal Atha Hamnais . . . . ?'

The porter shouted 'Ballyhaunis!'

We would hear that shout every summer for the next seven years but never again with Mrs Hayden. We must have seen her often when she came to Margaret's to ask for flowers for the friary altar, but my last picture of her is going down the station path between the carts and cars, erect as if it was her own private domain. When she saw who had come to collect us, her Merrion Square manners returned.

'Give her a dart of them stoneens!' Brod called back to us as he drove down behind her. 'Hi! Do not!' He pulled his head back as we scrabbled in the gravel washing up and down the floorboards. It was a little blue lorry, falling to bits. From the back we could see over the town. The train pulled out and we saw on the other platform a dozen men, each with a suitcase, standing in a line before another giant 'Béal Atha Hamnais'.

'Many's the scelp she gave me in there then.' Brod put his head out of the window again as we passed the National School and attacked the hill. There was a cloud of blue smoke and Brod went into neutral and coasted back downwards again. Mrs Hayden went into her house without even a glance at us—racing uphill again, thirty miles an hour in second gear. Her door shut as we rolled back down again.

'Where did you get her, Brod?'

' Ye don't know him. He's Biesty. He's a big shot below in Ballindine. Stop where ye are.' Brod turned and went into reverse and quick as the swallows skimming alongside we flew to the top.

'She's slipping in third . . . .' He turned right ways again at the graveyard gate. Down the avenue of tombstones we could see, across a mile of bog, our train steaming towards Claremorris. We ran in neutral down a straight road through warm smoky air that plumed back our hair as we stood behind the cabin.

'Yip yip alloi! Ben Hur!'

'See can ye tip Johnson's mare beroad!' Brod stuck out his head, pulled it in again shouting 'Do not!' as the mare bolted into a quarter acre of green oats. More rain. The sky went bright grey. The swallows were skimming inches above Margaret's hair as she stood arms folded at the gate.

'Here, Brod, till I give you something.'

'Give me nothing.'

'Sure, I can't give you nothing.'

'Nothing in the wide world, Maggie!'

'Will I give you half-a-crown?'

'Well, I'll leave it to yourself.'

'What's he like at all? He's like a little nigger. Did you see the hands of him?' Margaret watched the blue cloud up the road, and then turned to look down, Nothing, and not a sound. It was as empty as the road in Dublin where our new house was. There were only smells: of oil from the lorry, clay from the garden, turf smoke that the wet gusts were driving down the roof, and the wet new tar under our sandals. She glanced across the road. Under a pair of big blue-silver willow trees, just above a potato garden as blue-silver with spray, was a long low thatched house showing through two notches cut in a hedge two little windows shining like eyes. Margaret turned and led the way, welcoming us home as we turned the gable.

'There's my Felix. Look at him watching you.'

'Where?'

'That's my cat. Do you see him? Beside the post. He doesn't

know who you are.'

'Have you a dog?'

'I have. I have him tied up.'

'Will he chase the cat?'

'No. He follows me everywhere. I just have to tie him up when I'm going out. I'll let you let him out afterwards.'

We stood chatting like that in the drizzle while the little birds, that had lifted from the weeds, skimmed back down to them again. My brother looked as if a great stone had been lifted from his back. He picked up a little stone and threw it in the air. It landed with a crash on the galvanised roof of the cow house and two pigeons clattered out of the trees behind. Through them we could see down empty fields that slipped out of sight and rose again a mile off as a long bushy hill. From there came a last whistle of our train. Two months of freedom before us! from weather forecasts and dark silences, our mother's groany whispers to the Sacred Heart and the rush of air as our father walked past us up the stairs.

Smoke flew out of the door when Margaret opened it. She was almost the same height as our father and her wavy hair, cut short, showed the same jaw. She towered over our grandmother, not much bigger than us, who only had to bend her head to press her cheek to ours. There was a different, lighter jaw, but the same heavy hooked nose—and a sharp tongue for Margaret, who bent for the tongs. Some embers had rolled off a heap on a pot oven and were smouldering on the lip of the hearth, filling the kitchen with smoke. It was small and stone-floored, with a low ceiling of plaster so thin, it was mottled with shadows like a duck egg. When Margaret stood up and yawned and stretched, it looked as if she would shove her hands up through it.

Grandma sat down to admire us and leant her stick against

the chimney. It was only the length of the tongs. She was eighty years older than me. Her hard little hand ran up under my shorts to feel the material and, when it felt something else, stopped and felt again. In class, only a few months ago, Father Lamont had asked us in turn if we wore underpants. I had never even heard of them. Father Lamont was tall and manly. One day he kicked Gibbons into the wastepaper barrel, and he spent all Sports Day with another boy's mother. The priests had given books of their own to start the school library and in one I found a snapshot of him as a young man with a beautifully dressed girl. He seemed so pleased when I showed it to him that I looked again, and found another. Soon everyone was using the library. After school, at the bicycle shed, the senior boys told us the stories he had told them: how he had been walking by the canal one night when a woman approached him. Father Lamont had stopped and talked with her and then—suddenly the senior boys whipped open their scarves—revealed his Roman collar. They had already heard the underpants story, but I told it at home and what Father Lamont had said: how they gave support and protection and, above all, they were clean. It was shortly after that I got mine.

As they did every year, Grandma and Margaret talked about who we were like. They did not know where my brother got his long yellow legs from. I got my hair from my great grand-uncle, William Flynn. Grandma could not pronounce my name—she said 'Aireen'—but I was used to that from the bus conductors who quizzed us on the way home from school. To make it worse, it was not my real name. I had been christened Thomas after my grandfather, but the priest had asked my mother if she did not want to give me a second name? His name was Adrian—the loveliest little priest, Mama said, with the most refined face (she pinched in her cheeks), a bit like Pope Pius. Everyone was like someone else to my mother.

Grandma took her stick and tumbled the coals off the oven

lid. Again with her stick she lifted the lid and a beautiful scent filled the kitchen. When we went upstairs to change our clothes, we met it again mixed with the turf smoke that hung in fleecy blue shingles at the top of the stairs. Through the square high rails you could see down into the kitchen below and through a small square window on the other side you could see down into the street.

The first thing we did when we opened our suitcase was to take out the gun. Our father had broken it open and had left it on top of our clothes. Underneath was a box of five hundred pellets, less a few he had used the previous evening showing us how to load and fire. His big fingerprints were still like stains on the barrel—a plum blue, with the name 'Diana' engraved in copperplate on the lock and the outline of the goddess standing tip-toe holding aloft an air-gun. We stood it in the corner beside our fishing-rods, also new but in an old case which the shopkeeper, a friend of our father's, had thrown in. It was stamped with a royal coat of arms and a DIEU ET MON DROIT you could read from the other side of the room, a big bare room. On the mantelpiece was a statue of Blessed Martin with his head at his feet. We put it back on but when we walked away it fell off again. The ceiling sloped down at either side, so the chest of drawers stood out from the wall and the mirror on top leaned forwards, reflecting the floor.

From the window as we undressed we could see our potato garden below, a hedge of sally bushes and then a meadow with a drain full of white and yellow weeds down the middle. We could see and hear a horse and cart going across the foot of this field on a raised bog road. The land sloped up then into a long low hill like a fish's back, with a hedge along the top like a fin, and just where the tail would be was a grey house in a handful of trees. We jumped into our old shorts and put our new penknives in the pockets.

In a few minutes we were at the top of one of our trees, looking down at the house. The trees were not like those at school. They were covered in moss that we had to peel off before we could find last year's initials and carve them afresh. We could see for miles, but there was no sign of anyone. We walked to the end of a branch and jumped off screaming, then halfway to the ground caught another branch, and so on until our hands were green and raw. When a guinea hen flew up onto the roof of our bedroom and began to scream, Margaret called us in to our tea. An ass brayed and our cow mooed and then the horse and cart, with a man standing in it singing, went up the road. We noticed the same thing next morning and soon got used to the small stir at the beginning and end of each day.

Grandma ate everything to the last scrap. When she had finished her boiled egg, she took it up in her hand and went over it again, then she broke it open and picked out more bits until her lips and lap were covered with flakes of shell. The caraway seeds in the cake she had made for us, that we cracked between the points of our dog teeth, she chased with her tongue and held between her gums until they were well sucked. She wanted to talk, but Margaret just wanted to hear us: what Mrs Hayden was wearing and about our new house and school.

My brother told her about a Spanish boy in his class whose father had only one arm. How he got a driver's licence I do not know, unless it was through being an ambassador. But Grandma was not interested in how sometimes he drove us down the school avenue at fifty miles an hour. Margaret interrupted 'Sure that couldn't be right. Sure how could he manage the gears?'

Grandma said, 'Isn't it equal to you.' Then she said, 'Take off my boots, agra.'

I knelt down and took off her boots and rolled down her

33

garters and stale stockings while Margaret sat listening. The Spanish ambassador did not only change gears—he made racing changes, slamming his shoe on the accelerator in the split second between gears and then his hand was on the wheel again and the empty sleeve of his coat was flapping faster in the breeze.

Grandma just yawned and set her small feet on the hearth to admire. Another of my jobs was to wash them every night. My brother's jobs were to go to the well and light the lamp. When he had the lamp hung back on the wall, Margaret got up and cleared the table. Before she came back, Grandma had begun a story. It was not that she just liked the sound of her own voice, although she was vain (I used to see her take a mirror out of her apron pocket and look at herself, especially her hair which was as silver as the mirror) but she liked talk only if she could join in, or if it was a story. If we could have told her the story of how the Spanish ambassador had lost his arm, she would have listened. But we couldn't, so she began one of her own stories. They all began in the same lighthearted way: 'Long ago, when pigs were swine and birds built their nests in old men's beards—' But when she got into the story, her voice was serious. It was about a man called Tom Comer who had a cat. Margaret got up and went up and down the stairs with a chamber pot, a hot water bottle, a cup of spring water and a rubber sheet, and then waited leaning on the jamb of the door until her mother was ready.

'Now, Tom—the cat said . . . .' Grandma lowered her voice to a nasty whisper and stopped see-sawing her chair. It was a rocking chair, but the rockers had been so good they once almost pitched her into the fire and Margaret had sawn them off, except for a couple of inches. The cat threatened to scratch Tom's eyes out if Tom did not get him a pair of shoes. In the end, Tom agreed and carried him to town in a bag. The bag grew heavier and heavier as they went and, when they were passing a lake, Tom tied a stone to the bag and threw it into the water. Before it sank, the cat leapt out spitting like a serpent and then—for some reason— dived head first into the lake.

They all ended the same way too: 'And from that day to this he was never seen again.'

'Now, come on,' Margaret said. Every night she had a fight getting her up the stairs. There was an old barrel of rain water outside the back door and a table and basin where we washed. From there we could hear Margaret shouting inside.

'Just lift your foot! Go on! Lift it up! UP!'

There was the full June moon rising high up in the sky. Margaret glanced out at it as she came into our room to draw the curtains and, as she did, we heard the noise of the train. It was the one we had come down on, she told us, on its way back to Dublin. We heard her go downstairs and then there was silence.

A different silence from that in Dublin. It was black, yet the sky was white with the moon and stars—and in the same way although the silence made my ears ring, it was filled with sounds. Just outside the window something made a tiny hiss like my mother made when she sucked a speck of food from between her teeth. A crumb of soot fell down the chimney and rattled off *The Far East* magazine crimped in the grate. Downstairs, Margaret's chair scraped on the floor. I pictured her taking the hairpin from the wave behind her ear and imagined I heard the scratch as she went over the figure 40 she had for some reason once cut in the right arm rest. She worked and re-worked it as absently as she smoked a cigarette and yet there was never a scratch astray. It was always the same perfect figure, as if it had been carved by the man who made the chair.

My brother fell asleep and slipped down into the sag of the bed. I lay awake on the slope.

S-S-S-Silence.

There was a boy in my class who when he was asked his

35

catechism one day knew none of the answers. Father Murphy had turned back a page and asked him something easier and, when he still did not know, had turned back again, and so on back to the very first page, then back up through the first page and finally to the very first question in the book: 'Who made the world?'

Everyone was praying he would not know, and he did not. He just stood looking down at his desk in silence—thrilling, heavenly silence like this.

3

Next morning we heard the train again and when we went down the fields after breakfast there was the railway embankment like a giant ditch across the bog. I had a stool to carry, my brother a bucket, and Margaret took Grandma by the arm. We went through a field of thin oats and a meadow full of thistles, stopping every minute while Grandma looked at something. She had not been on the land since last summer. Even the cow, who looked fat and happy, got her cold stare. It reminded me of Father O'Conor's. She clutched my shoulder while Margaret milked, watched for a moment and then turned to hit a weed with her stick, beating it until the yellow crown was in tatters.

'Glory be to God' she breathed out and looked about the sunny field. Through the gap I could see the river bending below us under a gold skin of weed.

'Tomorrow is the longest day,' I said.

'And it is,' Margaret said. 'And it's Corpus Christi. Isn't that queer.'

My brother said it was the feast of St Aloysius Gonzaga too.

'There'll be no work done at all so,' Grandma said.

'Wasn't it you always said even the bird wouldn't bring a bit to his nest that day?' Margaret said and put her two hands to it and drove the milk until it came up in foam.

Grandma let go my shoulder and turned back to the house. Margaret gave us the bucket to carry and hurried after her to take her arm, shoving aside with the milking-stool the tall thistles in their path. Grandma stopped at the gate for a last look. A hen strutted out of the oats and called that she had laid an egg.

'*Marbh fáisce*,' Grandma said and went back inside. I think that was the last time she ever went down the fields.

As the gate banged shut, a wren flew out of the pier and we found her nest, right in the hinge socket. Both the barn doors were open; they were red rotten and the wood dust lay heavy on the cobwebs. The swallows were flying in and out repairing their nests, but we could not reach them. We climbed the small sycamore again. There was a new 'Elsan' lavatory in the old duck-house but I found that perching on a branch that hung over the meadow was better.

'Let me catch that happening once again and it's the train back to Dublin,' Margaret said.

'Isn't it equal?' Grandma said.

'Where used you to go, Grandma?'

'In the bed of nettles. And wasn't it good enough?'

'And what if you got stung?'

'What, only to laugh.'

'And if somebody saw you?'

'Only to laugh all the more.' She saw Margaret smile again and asked us a riddle: 'Born without a night cap, christened without any skin, came into the world roaring and was never heard again. Who am I?'

'Who?'

'You rude thing,' Margaret said.

'A fart.'

While she said her prayers we washed the dishes. As we dried, Margaret told us how her father had added on the back kitchen when she was a girl, but how even now her mother would have nothing to do with it. She began to explain how building to the West was meant to be unlucky and then she let us go.

Rex was tied to an old piano in the cow house. He was an Irish terrier and his strong tail beat music from the wires as we untied him. He ran with us as far as the road and then lay down in the tar along the edge, whimpering and straining as if he was still tied. My brother loaded the Diana and we left him behind.

There was a wild wall of hawthorn and snowberry along the roadside, so it was all shaded. Through a gap we saw a field of rushes and halfway across a boy's head watching us. He jumped up and pulled up his trousers—no underpants—and ran. When we got to the head of the bog road we saw a tinkers' camp and there he was before us, and I remembered him. Last year we had begun to make friends with him; been taken into their waggon one day and shown a sweetcan full of balls. He could say where he got each one, pointing to a green rubber one and saying 'I got that in Ballinasloe'. He looked at us now but we passed by, up the road to Brod's house, the fish tail house.

Brod was nearly seventeen but he had not gone to England because he had a bad leg. His father, though, cycled for miles with a spade tied to the crossbar digging up young trees, anything up to six foot, that he brought home and planted. He had cherry, alder, beech, birch, even oak; the small ones splinted to broken handles of hay rakes or sheltered in bottomless buckets. Someday, I thought, Brod would be living in the middle of an impenetrable wood. But his father was making a big new entrance. He was standing on a turf barrow up against a new cement gate pier, lifting with his penknife sprigs of wooden moulding, and we saw underneath a small cement cross. As he turned to the other pier he saw us, looked at us, then down at the tinkers' camp. Every year it was the same—we had to remind everyone who we were.

'We're staying with Margaret.'

'Ye must be Eddie's lads.' His dog came over, wagging his tail, and he kicked him in the neck and said 'How are they all up above in the city?'

'Grand.'

'The dad gave you that—hah?' He took the gun and broke it open. 'He's a great dad so he is. How do you cock her?'

'There's a slug in her.'

His little groves of trees right and left were already limp with the sun. On the tip of a cherry tree sat a yellowhammer calling his Ch-ch-ch-ch-ch-ch-Chee every few seconds. Matt leaned against the pier and took aim. He had lost two fingers and pulled with the third. The yellowhammer called again.

'Load her up again.' He took off his cap, leant his white hair against the cement, held his wheezing chest still and fired again. The bird sat where he was and, after a few seconds, called again.

Matt bent down to cough and spit and my brother took aim and fired. The yellowhammer dropped into the long grass.

'Where did I get him, Matt?'

It was strange—in Dublin we did not know an adult by his Christian name, and here we did not know one, except the priest, by anything else.

A single tear of blood rolled down the yellow cheek. Matt tossed the bird away. 'As the Yank says—you drilled him.'

'What'll she kill at?' His brother came out, carrying a pair of trousers dangling a needle and thread. Brod came out from under the lorry. That was the way for the rest of the summer: everyone from Father Bentley, especially Father Bentley, wanted a shot at something. Brod picked a bullock across the road, a stocky black polly that just swished his tail as the pellet went home.

'Hi! Do not!' Matt looked up to Mannion's: no one.

'Here, give me again. I'll give him the mixture!' Brod reloaded and fired and the polly began to trot. Brod quick-loaded and this time must have hit the head. The polly turned and galloped. A fourth shot and he broke sideways out over a ditch, tearing barbed wire and stakes after him.

'By God, she's a dandy!' Brod rarely gave praise to anything mechanical. 'Was it the dad gave you that?'

'That's the man with the money,' Matt said. 'The green boxeen under the bed. And tell me—does he take a drink at all now?'

'No—'

A motor car came down the hill and passed by.

'Mannion.'

'He must have been above at Tarpey.'

'They must be great again.' His brother took the gun, holding it with the torn trousers in under his arm, and fired after the tyres. The pellet made a long low whine along the road and we each tried that again. Then another yellowhammer came along. We were waiting for a third and talking when the one o'clock train whistled in the distance and then passed before us, half a mile away across the fields and bog on its high shining road. Almost at once Matt's stomach began to rumble.

'You know where ye'd a right to go and it's paved with bloody jackdaws?' He pointed out the trees on the nuns' hill, just beyond the smoke of the train. They went into dinner and we turned back, down the bog road, along the river and over the embankment and the silver tracks and climbed the convent's hill.

We could see right across the country, yellow brown and cracked with turf banks and fossulas like an old pie dish. There wasn't a single child our age in any of the houses we could see, only in the tinkers' waggon and it would be moving soon—if Matt had anything to do with it, maybe to Dublin, maybe even to that field behind our house, our old house. I looked at my watch. Half one. My father would be having his dinner now, looking at his watch between each mouthful. Or maybe it was today we were moving and the van was on its way. Or maybe we had moved already .... There was Margaret, standing on a chair at the gable, shining the window panes with a ball of *The Western People*. Each time she turned to look up or down the road I could see the flash of glass. Beyond was the long hill, no longer like a fish-back. Now I could see the land rising behind, fold by fold up to the Galway border, where Mama came from—a dark horizon sprigged with trees like the tips of the feathers of advancing Apache hordes.

When we got to the top, the jackdaws rose up in a black cloud and called, then settled again. There was a heavy sweet smell of rabbits, and foxgloves were growing between the trees. It was my turn first. I put a pellet in the gun and a dozen in my mouth. The young birds had their feathers and they perched on branches above the nests chattering with the old birds.

'It's paved with them!'

'By God, she's a dandy!'

We took off Matt and Brod as we fired. I spat another pellet into my hand, loaded and fired again and down dropped another, stone dead. I couldn't miss. Each time a bird fell, the flock rose in the air, then circled down into the treetops again. My brother stood with his hands on his hips and his head back so far he had to open the top buttons of his shirt. There was one, rocking on a long jutting-out leafy branch like a long feather. Down he came, tearing through the leaves and thumped at my feet. One came tumbling sideways and clinging at the branches, the way we played when we jumped off the top of the syca- more—but losing hold. He rested on a flat hand of leaves, fell through and landed at the foot of the tree. He scrambled sideways and got his back up against the trunk and lay snapping his beak and flexing his claws.

'Great Scott!'

I pressed the muzzle to his breast and fired from the hip. Less and less of the flock rose as my brother had his turn. They sat on the branches with a few more arriving now and then back from the town and a few swirling and tumbling in play just above the treetops. We could have used up all the pellets standing in one spot; instead we ran through the little wood, picking shots. When we got to the edge of the trees and looked back, the ground looked as if it had been weeded and hoed. There were rough black heaps lying everywhere. When I broke open the gun and looked down the barrel, it was striped with lead marks.

We were both dizzy and bewildered. The disgust we felt was half fear. It vanished when, as we slid down the hill and across the railway tracks, the flock rose up out of the trees looking bigger than ever and followed us high overhead, calling.

It was two o'clock when we got home. There was a man's bike outside the gate with a greasy wisp of hay caught in the chain and a brass pump on the carrier, just like last year. Inside, our Uncle Petie was having his dinner, sitting as usual at the window furthest from Grandma and the blazing fire.

'How are they all at home? I say!' she called again from across the room.

'What?' he called back.

It was a fair day and his mouth, a thin upper lip and thick lower one, just like hers, was stained with drink. He had the same fleshy hooked nose and boney hands, only twice as big. Grandma tried again, her voice cracking as she shouted: 'Did you sell the calf?'

'The curse of God on that bitch's bastard . . . .' again in a voice she could not hear.

42

Margaret called in from the back kitchen, 'They're not used to hearing that kind of language at home.'

Petie sat around sideways to shake our hands, chatting to us and looking us in the eye as he squeezed—to see how much we could take.

'What?' Grandma cried and Petie softened and called back a bit of news: 'Toss Jordan is dead.' He admired his hands, as hard and brown as wood, while we caught the fingers in our fists and tried to wrench them back.

'Who'll have that place now?' Margaret called in.

'Aye-oh . . . .' Petie yawned, a yawn that took on a life of its own. He stopped for a breather, yawned again, then he said 'Have ye a drink in the house?'

'You have enough.'

He took a glass and gave it to me, saying 'Put a dropeen of spring water in that like a good ladeen.'

'And poor Toss is dead.' Little tears oozed out of Grandma's eyes. Petie went over to the fire and threw out half the water clumsily, scattering ashes out over her boots. Margaret opened the press, poured him some whiskey and called 'Will you have some yourself, mother?'

Petie emptied his glass and strolled out. We followed him, across the street, in one barn door and out the other, where he relieved himself into the ashpit. The swallows swept in both doors to the nests above the loft with sobbing kissing sounds.

'Have they young ones, Petie?'

In a fit of good humour, he went up the rotten ladder to the more rotten loft. A boot-sized bit of wood, light and crumbly as a biscuit, landed on my head. Petie's bony leg drew up again and, through the hole, I watched him stand on a horse collar and reach up to the rafters. His thinness made him look tall, in fact, he was just the same height as my father. The suit he was wearing, a light grey herringbone with a fine red dark stripe, was hanging loosely . . . and the hat . . . I recognised them suddenly— they were my father's! No need to ask where the boots came from. They came down now almost on my head as the horse collar and then a whole piece of the loft floor collapsed. Then, in a cloud of smothering dust and a new sunbeam, Petie was standing beside us with a nest like a plucked apple in his hand. The swallows rushed past us in red white and blue streaks as he held out the mud cup to us, packed with gaping transparent mouths.

'They're only scalthawns.'

'Will they be all right, Petie?'

'Why wouldn't they?' He put the nest on top of the cow stall. It fell off and he picked it up and scooped clumsily the blue scalthawns into it again and left it on a heap of mouldy hay. In the morning they were dead.

The days flew by. There were a few rabbit snares hanging on a nail and, before he left, Petie showed us how to set one. Then there were our fishing rods, and the Diana, of course, and our new penknives. Every day our hands were red with new blood. When he arrived again a few weeks later, we were bleeding a chicken, that Margaret had killed, into the ashpit. Petie looked at us, speckled with blood and ashes, and drew in his lips as if he was swallowing a belch—that was his smile: 'Ye're proper navvies now.'

4

Every year about this time, just before Austin arrived home, we seemed to have an almighty row with Margaret. It built up quietly and burst suddenly. One year it began on a Friday when I put jam on my herring. This year it was about a carving-knife.

It was a new knife Margaret had been sent from America with a nine-inch blade and a black wooden handle held by two brass rivets. She gave it to us one morning to cut a head of cabbage and we stood throwing it at one of the trees that hung over the garden. We managed to stick it a few times—then the handle hit the trunk and snapped off.

Margaret was angry but it was not until one of us said that the handle was just wood that the row began. She said it had steel down the middle and showed us the broken handle, like a sandwich with steel showing between the two slices of wood. We said that that was only a steel band set around the outside. Margaret made a stubborn trumpet of her lips and said 'No no. That's solid steel, right down the middle.'

'It isn't—'

'It is—'

All morning long, while the cabbage boiled to nothing, it went on. When we showed the handle to Grandma, she threw it on the fire but that only made everything worse.

'But when you looked at the broken end you could see' we said, 'there was just a hole for the blade to fit into.'

'No. I saw it. That was solid steel. Right down the middle.'

Grandma took out a ten shilling note and said, 'Buy a new one.' Then she took out a pound and shouted, 'Buy two!'

Margaret's face was shaking pale. Next morning, when she was raking out the ashes, we were right behind her and it began all over again. The handle had burnt, leaving only a bit of metal that could have been anything.

'Now look. It was only a band.'

'No, that's solid—' she almost sobbed—'solid steel.'

She had made us clean out the henhouse in the afternoon and had gone to bed. Once, when we rested on our spades, she appeared at our bedroom window, her white slip pressed against the glass, calling down 'You couldn't be finished!' and we went back into the shed until we had the floor scraped to the black clay with little red worms disappearing down through it everywhere. But at teatime, it began again—what had got into us?

'It was wood—'

'It wasn't . . . .' She stopped and did not speak to us again for the rest of the week.

We went out into the street. The hens squawked in the warm dust. Margaret came out and hung a pair of her big pink knickers to dry in the evening sun and went back inside and shut the door. We took the Diana and went out the gate and up the road.

Every morning we saw boys going down to the National School—it was still open—and in the afternoon going up the road again, playing football with a book or a bird's nest or a hedgehog. They all came from the other side of the fish back hill, but when we got to the top we saw no houses, just the road running down straight between fields of snuff-coloured scutch grass. When we came to the head of a sand road where the ashes of a bonfire still lay, we turned and went down between dusty hedges. We turned a bend and there at the next bend were two children our age.

The boy had a cut-down sailor suit that hung below his knees. The girl had a woman's black dress to her ankles. My brother began to laugh until the boy threw a stone that threw up sand at our feet.

'Umba! Umba!' My brother jumped up and down like a Zulu, one hand holding up the gun, the other under his shirt playing the tom-tom on his bare tummy.

Then a crouched-down dog came hurtling towards us, his nose stuck out an inch above the dust. My brother threw up the Diana and fired and the dog howled and ran back even faster and the boy and the girl disappeared. We never saw the girl again. (The next year Margaret told us that she had died of T. B.) But next day when we returned, the boy was there with two other boys. Brod was there too, lying on a ditch.

'Brod!'

'I'm waiting on my sweetheart!'

One of the boys came forward and asked for a go of the gun. I said, 'What's your name?'

'Butther and crame.'

'You look it.' I turned away; he was bigger that I.

'Say that to me face.'

'What's so special about your face?'

He shoved a shoulder against me and threw me on my back, got on top of me and drew back a fist above my face.

'Oh, the tinker's blow!' Brod said and shifted to get a better look.

But he did not punch and I scissored my legs under his chin and forced him back and then I was on top, grinding his hands into the gravel.

'Arra, you're no good, Tarpey,' Brod said.

'Lither midil! Give him the lithir midil!' The others were dancing around us shouting. Now Tarpey was hammering the points of his knees into my spine. I leaned forwards out of their reach until my face almost touched his. His teeth were rotten and he reeked of sweat and turf smoke.

'Do you give up?'

He gave me a butt with his shaven head. 'I'll set your ribs creaking.'

'You wouldn't set eggs, Tarpey.' Brod picked a Rennies box out of the ditch and said, 'Here's a targate for ye.'

I made it an excuse to escape and ran to set it on a gate pier. John Edward, that was his name, blew it to bits and smiled at me. I blew a Bisodol box to bits and smiled back. The ditches were littered with things for indigestion and we spent the evening riddling them with pellets and then lay chatting on the ditch.

One by one the others joined us. A girl cycling a man's bike underbar with a gallon can of paraffin on the handlebars stopped by. There was an older man too, who each time he saw a bee land on the furze flowers, took off his cap and caught it, broke it in two with his thumb nail and sucked out the honey. Mannion's car came by and Brod tossed the girl's paraffin and a lighted match across the road—the car flew through the flames and blew its horn and we chatted again. We were just on the other side of the fish-back hill. Up and down the dusky slope went an old man with a spraying-machine between a few ridges of potatoes.

'Aisy saved anyhow. Roll them down the hill.'

'Lave the bucket at the bottom—'

'Open the back door—'

'Lave the pot at the back door—'

It was full night when we got home but Margaret did not say a word, or next morning when we set off again.

John Edward had left school. The master had come up for him, they said, but John Edward had filled his pockets with stones and had climbed up a tree. He was as good a shot with the Diana. With him every day, sooner or later, something exciting happened. We went down to the river and dammed it. It was as simple as that. You just heaped up sticks and scraws and the water ran up over the bank and Matt's six sheep ran up the hill. We ran after them, got up on their backs and rode them down again. Even in the graveyard it was the same. We were there taking shots at the tin crosses on the tinkers' graves one day when we came across a man lying on a grave having his lunch. He had been mowing; his scythe lay beside him. All I had eyes for though was what stood up from his open trousers. He was not a bit put out. He crossed his hands behind his head and lay looking up at us, chatting about fishing—he must have seen us down at the river—and every so often looking down at himself, saying 'There's a fine trout for ye!' It was as big as a trout too by the time we left. As we walked away amongst the headstones, John Edward said, 'There's a fine cockshot for ye!'

He crawled across a few graves until he had a clear view,

then got down on one knee and rested the barrel of the Diana on the arm of a cross. Someone's prayer must have been answered. Just as his finger was closing on the trigger, the man got up, buttoned himself and took up his scythe.

The rest happened quickly. It was evening and we were going home. Two blackbirds were shrieking at each other in a cherry tree and we stopped for a last shot. It was my brother's turn. He fired and the blackbird fell, flapping. He put in another pellet to finish him off and fired—just as John Edward ran forward to wring the bird's neck and save him the trouble. There was a shriek, not the blackbird, and John Edward fell down, clapping a hand to his forehead. My brother had shot him point blank.

There were cattle under the trees sheltering from the midges. John Edward leaned against one of them and took his hand away and the blood ran in a sheet down his face. We were there until it was dark. Then John Edward went home up the hill, saying he would tell his mother it was blackbird's blood.

But the next day there was no sign of him. The day after Brod told us that he was in bed with a headache, and the next— Brod laughed as he told it—that John Edward had got up but had fallen down on the kitchen floor. The day after again, when our gate creaked, I froze with fear. But it was only Petie.

5.

The chicken was for Austin. It was too big for the pot oven and so we were given one last dirty job before we got ready to meet the train. There was an old pot oven as big as a basin under a gutter where the hens drank. We rolled it down to a trickle that came off the well, scoured off the rust with sand and rinsed it with water. By the time we were washed, it was buried in red coals.

Austin had gone to England when he was twenty and for the next twenty years no one had heard of him. We learned that much later. All we knew was that since we had been coming here on holidays he had been coming too. His face appeared out of the train as it drew into the station and there was another of those noses, but in a round red English face so that you hardly noticed it. You noticed his voice though. Heads turned to his loud Yorkshire accent as soon as we arrived in the pub.

'I know you—whoever you are.'

'And I know you and all.' Austin stared at the strange face for a moment and the strange face stared at him.

'And well I know you.'

'Are you Lyons then?'

'And you're not too damn far out!'

'Too damn well I know you—' Petie turned impatiently from the counter and put an end to the guessing. But then it was our turn.

'And whose lads are these? Sure you never married, Austin?'

'No, mind you.'

'There's Eddie's lads.' Petie interrupted again.

'What Eddie?'

'Musha, our Eddie. And a couple of bottles of pop.' Austin put his hand in his hip pocket, where it spent the next fortnight. In the two weeks he must have spent his fifty weeks' wages. I thought he carried it all in that hip pocket, until I saw him one morning refilling it from his suitcase.

'Well, many's the night we spent in this same house—'

'Who?'

'Eddie and myself.'

'Sure, Eddie never drank.'

'Well, he'd drink you under that table. Do you see that table—?'

We sat outside on Austin's suitcase, smudging out the Customs' chalk marks. Not a soul on the long sunny street, except for one man drunk on the low parapet of the bridge. Now and then he lifted his head and took up a bell from the path between his shoes and gave it a clang.

'Roll up! Roll down! Roll any fucking way you like!'

' Go home out of that, Deignan!' someone shouted from the shade of a door.

We play-acted to the empty street.

'Roll up! Roll down!'

'Roll any fucking way you like!'

'The curse of God on that bitch's bastard.'

'They're not used to hearing that kind of language at home.'

'And a right good crossing it was—'

' No' my brother corrected me. 'And a right good crossing it *were*.'

Austin came out with two more bottles of lemonade and we passed another half-hour. The latest craze at school was magnifying glasses and, when I had asked, I had been given one. Not an ordinary one. I remembered the day before as well as the day I got it. I had been sitting in an armchair when my father came home from work, looked at me, said 'What are you looking at?' and clipped me across the ear. It was still ringing next day when he brought me home this glass. He must have got it in one of the antique shops he was always dropping into. It had a hexagonal ebony frame carved with tiny vine leaves and even tinier bunches of grapes. From two grooves in the rim, silver legs unfolded to form a handle. Father Hillery had taken it from me in class one

51

day and looked surprised when, at the end of term, I asked for it back. Not half so surprised as I, when he came down the stairs and put it back in my hand.

There were ants teeming through the dust about the suitcase and with the glass we set ambushes for them, farthing-sized circles of burning heat. We bombed their rear and flanks with spits to cut off retreat, but there was no need. As soon as one vanished in a wisp of smoke, another arrived, like the jackdaws, drifting in over the town now for the scraps we heard being scraped from plates behind the long sunny street.

No bike for Petie today. He knew what was before him and had come by ass and cart. The ass was tied to the telegraph pole, so tightly and high up that his muzzle pressed against the DANGER KEEP AWAY plate. Austin took his time undoing the knot, chatting about some other old ass as he handed in the reins to Petie lying on the floor, clapped him on the back, then clapped the ass. The ass set off and the humming black veil of flies about his head followed, out the country road, home.

That was the word we heard most. Like us, Austin was home for the summer; but, when we got home, we knew that home was really somewhere else. Through the sycamore trees behind the house, we could see the long bushy hill behind which Petie was being drawn by the ass who knew the way home. That was the house where Grandma had lived and where her children—Margaret, Petie, Austin, our father too—had been born. Somehow, we did not know why, she had moved with Margaret to this house, leaving Petie to farm in the old house that everyone called Home. This house we just called Knockshinny like everyone else, except Mrs Hayden, who called it Knockshinny Cottage.

The burnt bit of metal was still lying on the wall outside the back door. As we followed Austin inside, the row ended. He bent to kiss Grandma, then kissed Margaret and then sat down to dinner, to the chicken she had killed with the knife without the handle.

'Will you have the wing?' she said to me, knowing how I

loved it. My brother's face looked suddenly as it had the day all his school lunches were found heaped rotting behind the chest of drawers.

******

Austin spent the first week of his fortnight with us. After a couple of days, we were used to his loud voice and the late nights and to the wireless turned up higher. In one of the programmes there was an advertisement that began 'There's one thing in life that none of us can do without—'. The announcer paused dramatically and Austin's voice drowned his—'Money!'

When he came back from town at night, he emptied his loose change onto the dressing-table for us to collect in the morning. We put it into the little drawers on either side of the bent-forwards mirror. They filled until we could not shut them, but he still poured out coppers and silver every night. 'Now, a jolly old sleep' he said as he undressed but, when he got into bed between us, he lit another cigarette and began to chat. We could hear Grandma and Margaret turning in their beds in the next room. But, even without Austin, it was noisier now. Just up the road a friend of Brod's was home from England. He had hired a car and, all day from eleven in the morning until dawn the next morning, he was burning up and down the road. The cottage across the road had an apple tree and kept a dog tied to it. Every time the car passed, the dog began barking, straining and straining until his collar throttled him. By the end of summer, he had every apple shaken to the ground.

As soon as he had finished his cigarette, Austin turned on his side and, before the red crumbs in the ashtray were out, he had fallen asleep. As soon as he woke, he reached out again. When he was digging the potatoes, he rested his cigarette on the ridge beside him. After dinner, he went down the fields until tea-time and we would find him, like one of the rabbits we had hunted with John Edward, sunning himself in a space between the thistles and the furze, or up against a ditch under the sloe bushes and woodbine, his own packet of Woodbines and a box of matches an inch beyond his outspread hands. He lay like that for hours, still, except for his lips. Even between cigarettes they moved. One day I was close enough to hear: 'Lirrely lie-di-die-di-die-di-di Lirrely lie-did-i . . . .' a tuneless whisper. Not a word from the other side of the fish-back hill.

But all the time the talk kept returning to next week when he would be going Home. If, say, we caught a frog and Austin was around, he would stick a straw up its behind and try to blow it up (he never could), telling us how he used to blow them up when he was a boy at Home. Then he would think of something else he needed for the journey. He ordered a half-barrel of stout. Then he remembered the tap. Then Margaret remembered that she would have to bring a clean dishcloth. After last Mass on Sunday he ordered the hackney car for the next morning.

Grandma had had little time for Margaret since we had arrived, less again since Austin had arrived and, now that the hackney was coming to take her out Home, she had none at all. Margaret had washed her and dressed her in best black and had brushed her hair silver shining and set it up in combs. But Grandma had got to the hall door by herself and, holding onto the doorknob while she waited, she straightened her back and held her stick lightly. It was easier now to believe the stories Margaret had told us about her: how with one blow of the churn-dash that broke its back she had killed a cat that had killed one of her chickens; or how, stripped to her slip and down on her knees, she could reap with a sickle better than any man with a scythe.

'No wonder you go nowhere.' She turned impatiently each time Margaret appeared behind her. 'You can't dress yourself.'

'I should have gone from you anyhow,' Margaret said, half to herself in her compact mirror. She dashed powder on her face.

Grandma took a step on her own, a crueller reply. We caught her arms and walked with her down the path, stopping each time she squeezed our arms and leant to one side to scent a flower. She leaned against the car and turned for one last look at the house—'Oh, the height of them sycamores'—as if she was

54

leaving it forever.

If only we were. Every nice thing that happened weighed down my heart more, like my pocket dragging to one side with all the silver Austin was giving me. By now he was handing money out like the balloonist casting off ballast in *Around the World in Eighty Days*. That was one of the books I had been reading in the parlour since John Edward had disappeared. Another, Charles Kingsley's *The Heroes*, had just arrived from my father. And then, at the last minute, we were told that, for the first time ever, we could spend a night or two out Home.

My brother got in, Austin got in. Then, just as Margaret lifted Grandma's little black boots in off the running-board and slammed the door, Brod appeared. His bad leg made corkscrew turns as he hurried down the road. I dragged my legs to meet him. He had a new job, he said, down in the town as a motor mechanic.

'How's John Edward?' I said.

Brod was late for work—late on his first day! he said—so he told me hurriedly. The doctor had lanced John Edward's head and had taken off a pint of pus and the pellet as well, and he was well again.

I hurried alongside. 'Are you sure?'

'As sure as there's a body on my head!'

Tommy blew the horn.

We stopped to collect the half-barrel and Austin stood a round of drinks and when we reached Knock—another. It was getting near to the Feast of the Assumption (my birthday and the reason for *The Heroes*) and the shrine was dressed. There was the Virgin standing at the gable in a bank of roses and potted palms as high as her crown. Oh holy, kind, wonderful, merciful, good, generous Virgin! I praised her under my breath. Austin's voice was getting louder as we got nearer Home, talking about one of the men who had seen the Apparition, a sore little briar if ever there was one, he said.

Tommy said, 'Sure, you never knew him, Austin?'

'I were only a nipper, like, but I knew him. Ooh, a right sore old devil!'

Tommy also could be sore, but he was too worried about his tyres now to argue. We had left the tar road and were going up a stony sloping road. The car began to roll like a boat. The brass tap slid across the dashboard and knocked over Tommy's luminous statue of Our Lady. Then the barrel began to pitch about in the boot.

'There'll be a head on that when we land abroad!' Tommy smiled.

'And not one drop of it will you ever taste, ferret,' Grandma smiled when he got out to have a look at it.

On our right the lake was breathless calm and far away on the left we could see the shape of Croagh Patrick, a pale blue pyramid with a mountain of white cloud balancing on top. Every year Austin asked the same questions. Grandma told him again about his grandmother who had lost all her children at birth, until in desperation she had set off walking one morning—

'To Knock,' Tommy interrupted agreeably.

Grandma breathed down her nose.

'Sure, there was no Knock that time,' Margaret said.

'Sure, that's right.' And Tommy, like the rest of us, looked across at the pale shape where Great-Grandma had walked barefoot. The next year she gave birth to a son—

'Father,' Austin said.

'John. And then your father.'

I cried every year at that and the pale shape dissolved. Without it, there would have been no grandfather to have my father to have me. But not this year. My brother nudged me with his elbow.

Tommy butted in to point out a bog hole he had hidden in when he was on the run from the Black and Tans. Then dogs began to attack his tyres. He slowed down and let them get ahead, opened his door and hit them flying.

'Powerful weather for Knock.'

We all agreed to that. The road was dividing and narrowing like a root until we were in a grassy track with briars rearing up against the bonnet. Around the bend and there it was before us—Home! a brand new bungalow on a raw apron of crushed sand and gravel. Petie was standing in front squinting into the sun. It did not face the same way as the old house behind, or any of the other white gables we had passed along the road. The old house stood a few dozen yards behind with a meadow growing on its thatch and, right behind it, like the end of *The Pied Piper of Hamelin* story, was a small green hill.

Petie helped with the barrel and Austin and Margaret linked Grandma to the new red door without even a glance at the old house. Inside, there was still a smell of fresh plaster and paint, just like our new classroom at school. A new top had been nailed to the old table, yellow plastic with gold flecks in it, shining except at one end where Petie's cup stood in a puddle of tea and breadcrumbs. The half-barrel was set on the chair—I recognised it, its red leatherette seat and brass studs all about, from one of my father's shops.

'Take it easy now!'

'Have you no right hammer?'

'Give us the tap.' Petie winked at me and dandled the sledge like a pencil. 'I learned this technique at college.'

A streak of stout hit the ceiling and then the tap was tight in the bung hole. But no matter how tight, it still dripped—like a cow dying to be milked. That was the message Petie gave us to bring to half-a-dozen houses he pointed out: 'The black cow's milking tonight.'

We guessed what it meant and I was MacDonald Hastings, *The Eagle's* special investigator, and my brother was Harris Tweed, extra-special agent. We were on a mission in Offthe-mapua, strolling tight-lipped past houses Petie had fallen out with, then slipping through a bedstead gate, past a stinking nettle bed . . . a dog with fits tied howling to a cow-house door . . . up to a dark cool kitchen doorway where a caged goldfinch sang.'Austin's home. The black cow's milking tonight.'

When we got home, the kitchen was full of women. Grandma was in Petie's chair, which had been Granda's chair. It was built up now with cushions, like a throne. Sitting on a stool was a woman with a face as black as her shawl, smoking a pipe, her legs apart like a man. It was amazing what you saw if you sat still and watched. She had a hole, a big hole, in one of her stockings. She saw it as I did and licked a finger and quietly reached up into the chimney and then rubbed soot on the spot and it vanished.

'And if anyone offers you a cigarette, just say "No thank you, my father doesn't want me to smoke just yet", our father had said to us before we had left. Margaret said it to us again that evening before she and Grandma left for home. In the same voice she said to Petie, 'And I don't want them sitting up with grown men drinking either.' We had heard that before too. It was good enough for Petie and we were sent to bed at nine o'clock.

Yet it was Petie who had persuaded her to let us stay in the first place. Through the chimney-breast we could hear him and Austin talking in the kitchen. Through our bedroom window, we could see the swallows still shooting in and out of the door of the old house behind. We hadn't killed them; just waited at the door with a sack we threw as they passed and the weight brought them to the ground. After carrying them around in our shirts for a while, we threw them up in the air again, and they just continued to climb, up to where the flies were crowding above the small green hill.

All the time the door was opening—we heard the music of hobnails on the cement—and closing. The noise on the other side of the chimney-breast stayed the same, like the murmur on the other side of a confessional. We read side by side in a big single bed until it was dark. I was reading *The Heroes* and I fell asleep dreaming of Perseus girding on his sword and his winged sandals and jumping off the cliff; and instead of falling, as he had feared, he floated as Athene had told him he would and he ran along the sky.

There were no curtains on the window and I woke early.

There were the swallows again, as if they had been flying in and out of the old house all night. Austin's door was shut. The parlour was open, although except for a single set of bootmarks across the raw floorboards, it looked as if it had never been entered. There was a new table and china cabinet and, side by side, on the wall two framed colour photographs of San Francisco.

I went into the kitchen. Petie's new china glasses, cream with red and gold bands, were everywhere—on the table, under the chairs. There was one brimming over under the dripping tap. Then I saw Petie lying on the hearth and—I thought of John Edward—I went cold. He turned on his side and grunted and lay still again. He was only drunk! Then I noticed a cushion under his head and his overcoat spread over him, and it dawned on me—he had given us his bed.

Outside the birds were singing—the same few songs echoing from everywhere. Petie's dog, chained between the shafts of the ass cart, began barking hysterically, leaping forwards until the cart stirred. The piebald mare limped through the litter of old bean tins and Milk of Magnesia bottles already building up outside the new back door. Petie had bought her from a tinker and kept her hobbled so tightly and for so long that the flesh about the ties was rotten. I smelled it as I passed. I went up the little hill. From the top I could see across the country to Knock, still sleeping under a white sheet of dew, with the sun rising at the end.

Afterwards, even after I had learned that my father had built this house, that was what I thought of when I heard that word Home: Petie's sleeping face before the huge fire that had burnt down into a pale mountain of ash that one touch would collapse.

6

'Escallop?'

'I didn't—'

'Can't you take it' —My mother smiled up at our waiter and he turned his silver dish, biting his lips as he eased the steaming hot shell down onto my plate. 'That will be sufficient.'

'And Madam?'

Mama had to look up again.

'How lovely!' The woman at the next table caught her waiter by the wrist and made him repeat what he had said. He had told one of her children not to be bold. 'Darling . . . .'

Her husband had a big book leaning on his sideplate. Today it was *Flora of the Maya Region*, full of slips of paper he wrote on with the propelling pencil he kept in his shorts. Every day he came to lunch in those khaki shorts, like ours, that cut into his strong khaki-coloured thighs. You could see eyelashes the same colour as he looked up over his glasses.

The waiter said 'Don't be bold' again for him and went away. Their two children were about my brother's and my age. The boy said 'I expect he means "cheeky"' and the girl said 'Precisely, Peter' and then they all laughed.

'Turn around' my father murmured.

'I don't like this.'

'Then don't eat it,' he murmured through clenched teeth. *'Leave it on the side of your plate.'*

'Isn't there something rather similar in Lancashire?'

Their voices seemed deafening. Some days they were away for lunch, but then the family on the other side took over. They were English too. Then at dinner the others were back, bathed and properly dressed and talking about a currach trip to some island or a mountain climb as if it was as ordinary as our afternoon drive.

My mother sipped her glass of water again, looking through

it like a telescope.

'Isn't she the image of Sister Victor over there?'

'Where?'

'There under the picture.'

'Which one?'

'With the wooly stockings and the flat-heeled shoes—the little Proddy one . . . .'

The crimped napkins reminded her of the scallop shells. The coffee reminded her of Lourdes. The window seat reminded her of the big house near her home and that reminded her of a day forty years before, when the landowner, seeing her father take a short cut across his park, rose from his window seat, opened the window and called 'You there! Come back here!'

Her cheeks went pink.

'And did he?'

'Meek as a lamb . . . Lewin was their name.' That reminded her of some long old rhyme:

'Lewin you growler your name is Towser

And Towser will be for evermore

You wear a rattle among the cattle

And eat Champions by the score . . . .'

' He said *that*! '

' This is when he got home . . . .' She raised her glass again. The woman in the woolly stockings was standing up.

I could picture her stories now, because on our way here I had seen her old home. Home, Home and Home again: there were as many as there were sips of water in the glass jug. This one was only a dozen miles up the road from Margaret's. Fifteen minutes driving and those sprigs along the horizon were tall beech trees among broken high walls. No use her stories about the great names who had lived behind them—Blake, Bodkin, Lewin, Kirwan . . . . Her hands, clenching smaller and smaller as we drew near her own home, told a different story. No help from my father either, except an occasional 'That's gone for the milk' as we passed another ruined triumphal gateway. This was demesne country. Apache country, I thought as we crossed a

61

small bridge and half-a-dozen children in boots and brown faces jumped off the wall and ran shouting alongside our car up to— not a white envelope glowing pink behind a Sacred Heart lamp, but a grey-faced farmhouse among outbuildings, shorn sheep, our uncle and, of all things, a young woman. We had not seen one of those since we left Dublin. She was taller than Mama's brother; their children took after her, I thought. A glance from her quick dark eyes and they advanced in a line holding out big hands to shake ours. Another sort of glance: our mother was advancing through the line to embrace her own mother.

Two months in Margaret's house, but only two hours in this one: a holy picture, a shotgun on the wall, a window at the end of the room where our mother sat talking to her mother in a low voice. Another of Josie's glances and our uncle put his hand in his pocket slowly and gave us . . . sixpence! between the lot of us! A flash of teeth then in a smile and we were getting back into the car. 'We'll see you again!' They sounded as if they meant it. Another fifteen minutes and the trees had fallen behind us, sprigs along a dark eastern horizon as we drove into a blazing sunset. 'She's lovely teeth,' my mother said.

'Everything all right?' The manager rested his fingertips on the edge of our table, leaning to chat for a moment, and then took the good out of it by turning and leaning over the next table.
'. . . Mr Oldman?'
So that was their name.
'We'll be getting down to first names next year . . . .'
He'd said that to us too.
Mama raised her glass again.
Through open windows I could hear the sea on the shingle. We were in a place called Renvyle—the bare point, Mr Oldman said it meant.
Mama put down her glass and caught my father's eye and traced a fingertip down the bridge of her nose. I knew what that meant. Jews. My father shut his mouth and shook his head slowly right to left and back again. I studied Mrs Oldman's nose

and jewelled bracelet, his fat bottom and the children's brown eyes as they all rose from the table.

'*Je me leve, tu te leve s'* Mr Oldman said. 'What say ye we tackle one of the Bens?'

'Rather!' Peter said.

'Isn't it lovely weather?' my mother said the next day.

'Rather!' Mr Oldman said.

'Such well-mannered children,' Mrs Oldman said the day after that. Like that, we grew friendly.

'The chocolate mousse?' Our waiter leaned in amongst us again. We sat sometimes talking until he advanced to clear the table. Our mother wanted to hear everything about our holiday; she seemed to know more about our father's home now than about her own.

I had called Grandma cruel when she told me how she used to bring a hundredweight of flour from town on the ass' back and sit on it as a saddle. When she added 'And I'll go bail he trotted that five miles home', I had started to cry—until she gave me the cold stare she gave the cow, and Margaret sometimes, and sneered 'Is it to feel sorry for the ass? Well, indeed!'

'And at the back of it all, of course,' Mama said, 'she's as refined. Tell me has she that green scapular yet that I got her from Sister Victor?'

'Petie has one anyway.'

We told her about Petie's new dog—he never gave his dog a name—that he was training to take tinkers by the throat.

My father closed his lips and shook his head slowly again.

Sometimes, when we left the dining-room, the hotel was empty: every G.B. car gone from the gravel; not a sign of life except the lounge turf fires smouldering and open novels left upside on couches, as if the place had been abandoned. Then, leaving the hotel to the waiters and following roads out along other lonely bare points, we would pass and repass the same cars. We grew used to seeing the sea swell on either side of us and, when the road ran out, to seeing it full before us.

'That's what you never told me,' Mama said. 'How did you get on with Mrs Hayden?'

We lied about that for a while, looking out at the ocean, an empty heavenly blue. A wasp drifted in the window. In the car his buzz was as loud as the engine. It stopped.

But none of us had seen him fly out again.

'Jesus!' Mama screamed. 'I feel him. He's on me.'

Then we each felt him, crawling over our skin, deep under our clothes. We got out and shook our clothes and searched the car. No sign. We left the doors open and walked the rest of the way to the point.

Another day when we had reached the end of the point, we continued walking with my father out to a rock and, from there, watched a cormorant fishing from a further rock. We were so absorbed by what we saw through the big Kershaw field glasses— the cormorant caught an eel and swallowed it and then the eel began to struggle back up the cormorant's gullet, we saw its head appear, vanish again and then the cormorant began to writhe like an eel and Dada told us that the eel was probably trying to eat its way out—that we never saw the tide coming in around our rock. When we did, it was so deep my father had to wade ashore, taking us one at a time in his arms.

Further and further afield each day we drove, until I got car sick or we came to some ruined castle or chapel or hotel.

' . . . passing south through Clifden from Galway, the wayfarer to Roundstone will note to his right a low whitewashed house, its extension and stabling. From its sheltered eminence on a tongue of land and framed with elm trees the windows scan a grassy . . . .'

'Sacred Heart ! Who is he at all?'

'Proprietor and manager Oliver St George Hawksley—'. My father put down the brochure. 'Well, it's *clean*. That's one thing.'

'All I want is a cup of tea.'

'Can I ring the gong?' I said.

'Sit down like a good boy before I ring your ear.' My father sat down and doodled with a dangling toecap on the carpet. He

64

still had that scar, I noticed, where—as he rushed me back to the car after another of my vomit stops—a briar had ripped his forehead open in a fine red line like those he drew under his long ledger tots. Then he had burst into tears.

The chapels we visited were as empty as the castles and hotels. Sometimes the tabernacle door was open and the Sanctuary lamp out, as if in Lent. It would be a chapel of ease. When I knelt down, the smell of poor Sunday clothes was still in the bench before me. Some chapels were so poor, they had not even a statue; only the crucifix over the altar. When Mama knelt down, her sigh echoed like a groan from the bare walls. Once, when she could not find a single slot to put money in, in desperation she left it in the dried-up holy water front.

Until the weather broke—a day with dark cloud hanging from the mountains and mist shining the gravel. We were going fishing. There were trout in the lake by the hotel and we had caught a few. But they were not *fish* any more than the perch we had caught with Petie. *Fishing* meant fishing for one of those salmon, or a sea trout at least, which were laid out some evenings by the manager on a silver tray in the hall. The men who caught them were already finishing their pipes, up to their knees in tackle in the hall, when we came down to breakfast. They were English too. Everyone in the hotel seemed to be English, except the waiters and the maids and us, and another family from Dublin. We knew them; they were at school with us and their father had a big business in the same street as my father. Yet somehow we hardly spoke. The only conversation I remember was once when their father stopped as he passed our table and showed us a groove in his sports coat, just above his heart. He made a golf swing with the soup spoon, demonstrating how the stubble on his chin had worn the cloth away.

The road was like that leading out to Petie's house, but here the sand had been washed away, showing sheets of rock underneath. Jungles of rhododendrons grew up the slopes and, above them, yellow waterfalls shot off boulder shoulders of those mountains the Oldmans talked about over dinner. We turned down a side road steep as the mountain above, inching with the handbrake half on until we came to an elbow and turned in big gates. An avenue of trees fallen and half fallen in giant alphabet shapes led to a house as big. An old woman leaning on a thumbstick came out. My father gave her money and she said something, then he said something and she laughed. They both turned to look up at the house, talking and then went inside. A few minutes later he came out swinging a key on a bit of string.

We fished all day and caught nothing. We lost one of the oars and had to drift down the lake after it, through the reeds and into rocky shallows. The lake was deep between two mountains, with the wind like a wall at the end. An hour to row up and the drift down only lasted twenty minutes. Up and down on waves the same brown and cream as the waterfalls above; no sound at all except sudden falls of shale down the mountainside and my father's curses as the wind whipped the cast into a bird's nest at the tip of his rod. We were soaked, but next morning, after his phone calls to Dublin, we set out again. We bumped into him, he bumped into us, in our eagerness to get the tackle together.

The vein that stood out sometimes from his temple like a small spur and ticked like a pulse had gone. Sometimes too, while he was driving, he spoke to himself under his breath, nodding his head, with his jaw stuck forwards. But now he was talking to us, joking, bending his head to look out, up at new waterfalls that roared above the noise of the engine down onto the roadside.

Today there was a man waiting to gillie for us. He rolled his cigarette to the corner of his mouth and began to row, looking through us down the lake, not speaking once. I sat in the stern watching the red end of his cigarette being whittled by the wind to a tip sharp as a pencil. When little half-starved trout managed to hook themselves on the troll going up, he unhooked them and threw them away like his cigarette butts without a word. We did not speak either. We were as silent as if the wind cutting over the mountain was Mr Oldman's loud English voice. Until there was

66

a swirl that parted the water by one of our casts. I saw a silver flank and then a bulge of water as the fish turned down, away out of sight. I began to cast wildly.

'You're not threshing oats, you know!' my father cried.

'Willie rose a big salmon there yesterday . . . .' Lazy and mysterious as the salmon, the gillie rose into conversation.

His name was Festy and, as we drifted past a cleft in the mountain, he pointed out his home. As he chatted, I thought of Petie—he was not too unlike Festy—and of the morning he walked back with us to Margaret's. He had the ass and cart but that calf he was trying to sell was in it, skidding about in his watery green dung, so we had walked too. Petie spoke only twice. Once, when I threw a stone and by a fluke killed a green linnet bathing in the dust on the road, he had smiled and said 'You don't need no gun'; and a few miles further on, when we passed a new bungalow just like his own and he looked across at the windows with the curtains still closed and —he gave his swallow-a-belch smile — said 'He's up there now with one hand on each of them.'

It was only now as Festy pointed out another speck he said was his wife I guessed what Petie had meant. Only because Father Hillery at the end of last term had brought into class one of the fretwork figures he made, of a woman with a bust—' Bust! a perfectly ordinary English word' he flared when someone sniggered—as huge and pointed as the papier mâché cones he used in Geometry class. And the only reason Father Hillery was in mind was because my father had brought us down our school reports—good marks for everything in mine (99 in Latin from Father O'Conor) except Geometry—39. Imagine failing someone by one mark . . . and I thought of that magnifying glass again.

The rod case rolled from side to side at the bottom of the boat. It had been covered in calf dung from Petie's cart—the royal coat of arms was gone for ever now, and with a splash of stout from the empty barrel. I thought of Austin, by now on the boat back to Yorkshire for another fifty weeks . . . . And so on, sleepy mechanical as the flies I drew and cast before me.

The tall alphabet trees bobbed past and Festy talked about

all the clay his grandfather had carted to plant them in.

'That was where Gogarty made the mistake—he wouldn't give nothing.'

Festy explained how Gogarty had refused to deal with the IRA.

'I never liked his kidneys myself,' my father said.

Festy told stories about our hotel and the goings on there in Gogarty's day: women without clothes bathed in the moonlight; Yeats cut stars out of brown paper and stuck them on his wife's forehead before she went to sleep. My father shook his head again. He did not like Yeats's kidneys either.

We had lunch in the car and, through the wet windows, watched Festy go into the trees and then appear on the hill's shoulder, dwindling until he was the size of the speck that came to meet him.

Every August afterwards we saw that speck until one year there was a new gillie. He told us that Festy and his wife had gone. A few years later we heard that they had not gone together. They reckoned there was faults on both sides, the new gillie said. They had not had any children and one morning they left their house together and locked the door and shoved the key back under the door and then parted, one turning left and the other right. But, by the time we heard that, the white speck we used to see from the boat had faded into the hill.

Half the day gone and not a fish Then in the afternoon the sun came out and by evening all we had were burnt red faces. But we stuck with Festy. Next day—more sun and the next.

In the end, our holiday nearly over, it was Festy told us where we should go.

In the few fine days the mountain waterfalls had gone again, and so had the river they ran into, except for one last waterfall where it ran into the sea. The small green-brown foaming pool looked harmless. We would have driven away if another car had not arrived just then. A man got out and carried a folding chair down to the bank above the pool, then returned to the car and led down an old woman on his arm. She had smoked glasses and must have been blind, for he had to guide her hand to the handle of the rod and drop the worm into the water; worms, that's what she was fishing with.

A salmon jumped up out of the pool. I had never seen one so clearly before. He hung halfway up the white fall, threshing his tail and beating his gill fins like wings, but fell back down into the foam. If only he could see what I could from the other side of the bridge, I thought: dry rocks with trickles of scummy water in between. Back to the other side again—just in time to see a sea trout throwing himself up the falling wall, and then a young eel not the length of a pencil but twisting like an awl until he drove up over the top and then he was like a bullet shooting under the bridge and out of sight. The pool was alive with fish dying to get upstream.

The man got back into the car, lit a cigarette and sat reading a paper, glancing down at the old woman now and then, getting out when she called. She called each time she had a fish—sea trout—which he landed and carried back to the boot of the car and then came back with a fresh worm. He looked up smiling as we approached. His aunt owned the fishing rights, he said, and after her holiday it was for hire. He smiled even more and said her holiday was over the next day.

We were there the day after and—Oh my God!—so were the Oldmans. It was the voice I heard first, words like 'gneiss', even above the waterfall's roar. They were on the other side talking to the bailiff, until he took one of the dried scraws he used for turf and went back into his hut. A billow of blue smoke came out the door and Mr Oldman moved away, still talking.

'. . . "Marteen"—it means "little Martin"' I heard him explain. Then I felt a tug at my line. I tugged back; there was a great pause. I felt a wild weight, like Petie's ass when he took the bit between his teeth, when we tickled his balls with the stick. The reel ran so hard, I could not touch it. I shouted and my brother came running and took the rod.

'Get the fucking net!' The first time I had heard him swear.

69

Where was my father? The car had gone, and the net in it. The salmon leapt out of the pool, back through the rocks and down the estuary towards the glassy green he had come from. I ran down the rocks.

'Steady on!' Mr Oldman shouted as I slipped on the seaweed. As I fell, I saw him loping up the slope, vaulting on the bridge down onto our bank, his 'Bunjy' shoes with their suction pad soles clinging to each rock he sprang on. Mairtín's head stuck out through the smoke, then the rest of him followed with a gaff.

'Mind the line!' another, even louder, English voice came over the water. The salmon was threshing between two sharp boulders that made a gullet at the end of the stickle. I dived after him.

'The tail! Get the tail. The tail!'

I recognised the kilt. It was Major Dundas, one of the anglers at our hotel. Sure enough, the tail was as firm as a wrist. We lay side by side, in a pool of water, the salmon and I looking at each other. Such an eye! With his other he must have seen the last white rush where the gullet opened to the Atlantic. Mairtín's boots came skating across the seaweed and a big rusty gaff reached over my shoulder.

'You're a bright spark, heh?' Major Dundas said. He pulled me up the bank and wiped his hand on his tartan bottom.

'A salmon!' My brother was almost crying with excitement.

'Grilse, actually,' Major Dundas said.

'That's the young salmon making his way upstream for the first time to spawn, Jennifer,' Mr Oldman said.

Mairtín upended the gaff. 'Mind out now, sir, till I give him the priest.'

'What's that, Marteen?'

'What the cobbler gave his wife, sir.' He knocked a silver dent in the dark head. 'The last, sir.'

'Oh, Marteen!' Mr Oldman doubled up with laughter. His hand went into his tight shorts pocket.

Mairtín said, 'Well, you're a gentleman, sir.'

Major Dundas walked away. Mairtín went back into his hut and only then did I realise I was shivering. I was dripping wet and covered with bloody grazes and salmon scales.

'If I were you,' Mr Oldman said, 'I'd cut along home. Where's your dad?'

Still not a sign of him and, in a few minutes, I was in the Oldman's car driving back to the hotel. There was no sign of my mother either, nor of our key, and in another few minutes I was in the Oldman's bath, up to my neck in the hotel's strange brown hot water.

The door was left open and I could see Mrs Oldman dressing for dinner. She had had her bath, the scent of her perfume was still around me. Now she was rubbing oil into her tanned and freckled chest. Mr Oldman strolled about, in only his khaki shorts now, rubbing his deep khaki-haired chest with one hand, holding a glass of whiskey in the other. Now and then he came in to see me, pressing my shoulders under the water, saying 'That's it' and strolling out again, still leaving the door open.

I had seen Jennifer's knees before, cut and scabbed like anyone else's, but only now I realised—as she took off her jumper— that she had a small, as Father Hillery said—bust. It was as strange as finding that I had two grandmothers. It was like looking at a play. They did not seem to notice me, even when they mentioned the salmon. Doors opened and shut. I was fascinated. Jennifer shut hers by stretching out a leg and tipping it with a toe, as she caught the bottom of her blouse and drew it up over her head. Peter was reading a magazine. 'What's *"nez?"* *"Nose?"'* he said, without looking up. Mr Oldman had another glass of whiskey and got down on his knees to study an Ordnance Survey map on the floor. Mrs Oldman lit another cigarette. I stayed there until the water was as cold as the river.

The hotel was crowded that night, There was a supper dance, 'In aid of Kylemore Abbey Restoration' the invitation cards said. On the back of one the manager wrote our names and

71

the weight of the salmon and set it on the silver tray by the hall door. The black-and-yellow eye had dried as bright as varnish. I could see it from where I sat in the couch by the fire, where Major Dundas and the others sat every evening writing up their angling diaries. Major Dundas had made me a present of a round silver metal box with a leaping salmon in relief on the lid; it was a cast-holder, and he was explaining what the lining was made of. It was something called 'amidou'.

Mr Oldman appeared and he began talking of amidou too. It absorbed moisture. My father appeared on the stairs, straightening his tie. He bought a drink-it looked like whiskey but I could tell from the bubbles it was 'Lucozade'. He joined us and then my mother appeared from the shadow of the stairs. She admired the gong. Then she took a few steps more and admired a painting and suddenly she was sitting beside my father.

Major Dundas was saying how when he was on the Nile they used to shoot the fish. Brass of a whole clip, he said, and there was one's supper.

'Go on,' Mr Oldman said. 'Who were you?'

'Gunners.'

'I see you have the scian dhu,' Mrs Oldman said, and Mr Oldman said, 'Look here, do you actually use it?'

Major Dundas shook his head.

Mr Oldman went on. 'It seems extraordinary, walking about with a knife in your stocking. What exactly is behind it?'

Major Dundas said, 'That psychiatrist fellow would probably come up with an intriguing answer—what's his name?'

Then my father put his foot in it. 'Frude?' he said casually. The silence seemed as long and deafening as the gong.

'Oh, you mean Freud!' Mr Oldman said.

I saw light between the couch and my father as his spine arched. Mama's mouth quivered—praying, I realised as the arrow flew.

'No no . . . .' Major Dundas said. 'What's that other fellow . . . .? Jung!'

Bong! The head waiter hit the gong. Bong! Bong!

But Mama's lips were still quivering. I shut my eyes. Oh my

God! She was going to shoot again.

Major Dundas's face coloured and he said suddenly, with venom, 'Can't stand that Jew—probing in the dunghill.'

Bong! Bong! Bong!

Major Dundas got up and led the way into the dining-room, his kilt swinging gently from side to side.

We had had high tea and so had all the other children. Even the barman was busy in the dining-room tonight and we had the hotel to ourselves. First we played ping-pong, as the English children called it, and then one of them said, 'How about Sardines?'

It was like Hide and Go Seek, with Jennifer the one hiding. My mouth still had the taste of success and I walked straight upstairs, down a corridor and opened a linen cupboard—where she was. I hardly saw her. Her face was so sunburnt, only the white of her eyes showed, but she caught me by the hand, pulled me in and shut the door.

The strange part about the most exciting things is that you often remember only the beginning. The day Father Lamont kicked Gibbons into the wastepaper barrel, for instance, I can't even remember Gibbons getting out afterwards. Even John Edward: all I remember is his clapping a hand to his forehead and the blood; but the whole hour we spent under the tree— what were we doing? or talking about? I forget, and in the same way I forget the rest of the evening in the linen cupboard with Jennifer. But that night and next morning again I found I only had to lift my fingers to my nose to remember her.

Sitting in the back seat as we drove out of Connemara, I tried again: there was her scent—so persistent. I tried again as we came into Dublin, but the perfume had gone.

It was not until we were back in our new house for a few days I realised that the scent came from the hotel soap. It made no difference. As long as the bar my mother had taken lasted, I could sit in class, bring up my hand and bring back the whole of that last day from the first tug of the salmon to Jennifer's English voice whispering to me in the dark.

II

UNCLE PAUL

7

The first thing you saw when you went into Gorman's was yourself in a four-square mirror that filled the end of the hall. Then you got the scent of old money, a scent as distinctively beautiful as turf smoke; and, like turf smoke, I noticed, it clung even to your clothes. If the windows upstairs were open, and they were generally, a sharp clean smell blew down from the surgery. There was a sheet of cellophane over the wallpaper on the stairs. Even the paintings, large gilt-framed dark-varnished canvases of shepherds and ruined temples, were shining. Sometimes when he was examining me—Dr Gorman soon became our doctor—when I had undressed, he put the back of his hand, cool! on my chest and tapped it with the back of his other hand, moved down a few inches and tapped again, and so on around my ribs and up my back. Everything in the house looked as if it had been examined like that.

But I liked it in Gorman's. It was different from home. You never heard a loose floorboard creak suddenly overhead. Mrs Gorman never stood looking out of a bedroom window. She was always in clear view, baking, or polishing the brass plate on the gate until it shone like the mirror, or in the front garden pulling up dandelions. She had the knack of pulling them so the top did not break off, but the whole long dirty white root came up clean in her hand.

In a way Gorman was the first friend I made at school, before even Joss and Art. Some of us were throwing snowballs as we walked to the bus stop one winter evening at the end of my first term. Joss and Art were with us, Gorman must have been too—some exciting things you do not even notice; for a few minutes after we passed his house a car drew alongside, a shining black Prefect, and Dr Gorman got out, asked which of us had been putting stones in our snowballs and, when we each shook our head, said his Anthony's head had been ' quite gashed open'. He looked us one by one in the eye, then said, '*I believe you*' got back in his car and drove home again. That is the first I remember of Gorman, and the next—soon after we had moved house—we were best friends. One reason, I suppose, was that by then Joss and Art had left.

Today, however, this day I remember, Mrs Gorman was baking—talking with us, as she sliced trays of shortbread with quick, single strokes of her knife. Their little Lakeland terrier sniffed about the shining red tiles for a crumb, in vain. Dr Gorman had called him Laika after the dog the Russians had put in their sputnik. Some evenings we stood out in the garden hoping to see it orbit and one evening we did see something, like a match being struck off the sky. Dr Gorman said it was most probably a meteorite, but he held up Laika to see, just in case.

'Adrian—' Mrs Gorman set a plate of crisp hot shortbread triangles before me. Gorman just looked away.

'Anthony?'

Did not even shake his head. He was like that at school with boys who teased him, standing sullen until they came too close with a shove or a shoe and then closing his arms about them in a slow crushing bear-hug.

He had had a 'talking', he told me as we drifted down the road. Never clipped on the ear, say, as I was, he was sent up to the surgery to be talked to by his father; about *The Three Musketeers* today, a book he had borrowed from me, although Dr Gorman had forbidden it because it was on the Index.

'What was it like?'

'Not bad.' Gorman fingered his chin thoughtfully, as if he

was talking about the book. 'Where'll we go to? O Braonain's?'

It seemed strange to be wandering down the road in the afternoon instead of playing rugby. I had been dropped: some of the forwards had thighs now as thick as my stomach. Gorman had never been on the team. He was so clumsy that doing something as simple as passing a cup of tea he could spill it, hot!, right into his father's lap.

Small and old—he had been out in 1916—with longish silky white hair and very sharp eyes, Mr O Braonain chatted with us on the doorstep, drawing a yellow scarf tighter about his neck, asking me my name again and what golf club my father was in. He had been in the drapery business but had sold his shops and retired. *'Fáilte isteach!'*—and as we followed him inside he told us the proper Irish response, telling us then that O Braonain was at piano practice. We could hear that. Usually, while we waited, he chatted to us in Irish, unless it was about something important. Today it was Suez, in English. Everyone was still talking about Suez. I did not know anything about it, but Gorman did, of course. He talked of Nasser and Hussein as if they too lived down the road.

'What you're seeing, boys, is the last roar of the British lion. Anthony Eden and his gunboats can do, say, think what they like, but there is one in-con-tro-vertible fact—' Mr O Braonain drew back a yellow-and-black-blotched hand and held it like a microphone—'Colonel Gamal Abdel Nasser!'

'Oh, I don't know about that, Mr O Braonain.' Gorman paled.

'Gabh mo leithscéal,' Mr O Braonain said.

'I beg your pardon?' For Gorman could not stand Irish.

' What are you talking about?' The red flecks in Mr O Braonain's cheeks filled the rest of his face.

' Surely France is also the aggressor, Mr O Braonain?'

' Are you comparing France, *La Belle France*, to that ... *vulgar* crew?'

'But according to the latest reports French gunboats were shelling Cairo, Mr O Braonain. ' Gorman leaned forward, Mr O Braonain leaned back. I listened to O Braonain playing in the next room—*All through the Night*—and wondered how my brother was getting on. A boy in his class, Corcoran, had invited him to a party today, in his house in Temple Road. I had given him a cross-bar there, my legs going weak when I saw the size of the house. Up up up the granite steps my brother went slowly, his present under his arm, up up up and disappeared.

'*Críocnaithe anois, a Dhaidí!*' There was a tap on the door and O Braonain's gold curly head appeared.

There were not too many places to wander. Palmerstown Park was out: some strange old fellow hung around there, Mr O Braonain said. He went up with his blackthorn one day but could not find him. There were the school grounds, but O Braonain did not want to go there. He could be very particular: at gym, for instance, when he was undressing he folded his clothes along the ironed creases, rolled up his tie and fastened the end with a small gold safety pin he kept behind his blazer lapel. So today we drifted on down the road and into the tangle of lanes behind, O Braonain smiling as usual, explaining his family again: how his father's first wife was so long dead that her daughter's children were older than he, and he was their uncle.

'Then you're your father's brother!' Gorman was making a joke when I heard a click-clack sound, then a boy on a bicycle came spinning around the corner. I had never seen him before; it turned out afterwards he was the milkman's son. Black tossed hair, open neck shirt and an open overcoat cloaking the back wheel, he cruised alongside us, turning the front wheel until we were pressed against a back garden wall. He did not speak, just punched Gorman's large head.

No help. Down the garden and over the wall came the wireless boom of J.Ashton Freeman, imitating animal calls. The milk boy did not even get off his bike as he turned to O Braonain and twisted his arm behind his back. It was strange—even with tears standing out in his eyes, O Braonain seemed to be smiling. He had a wristwatch, the boy saw it, took it and put it in his pocket, then, looking Gorman up and down and saying for some reason, 'And *look* at his bloody shoes', he gave him one last punch in the head and cycled off down the lane and out of sight.

In school the next day, O Braonain told us the arrangements his father had made. Someone he knew in Dublin Castle was sending out a squad car to collect us, to drive us about the city to see could we point out the boy to the Guards. Gorman was so excited he forgot it was his day for going to the barber. When he remembered, he looked as if he had been punched in the head again. But his hair was so short this week, we decided to cut what had grown ourselves and say nothing to his parents.

After school we hurried to O'Braonain's and saw the black squad car outside. A Guard was sitting at the wheel, another in plain clothes was standing talking to Mr O Braonain, who had his blackthorn. I realised that he was coming too. That took a lot of the excitement away. We stood waiting for them. Then, casually, the plainclothes man turned to us and said, 'That's not him?'

We looked around. There was the same boy cycling the same bent-pedal bike out of the mouth of the same lane, whistling the same tune.

'Yes!'

And the boy saw us and the squad car and the Guard springing out and the plainclothes man and Mr O Braonain raising his blackthorn. He stood on his pedals. The plainclothes man ran after him—a frightening hammer of leather soles—and caught him by the shoulder. The bike flew on down the road. By the time it had crashed into some railings, the plain clothes man had opened the back door of the car, said 'Get in, you pup you!' and given the boy a punch that knocked him across the seat, almost out the other door. The boy began to cry, put up a hand to shield his face, and I saw O'Braonain's watch on his wrist. It was all over. The squad car drove away and my heart fell in disappointment. My chance of a drive through every dirty exciting back street of Dublin was gone, gone for ever like the watchstrap Mrs O Braonain burned for fear of germs. I walked home without even cutting Gorman's hair.

Do I remember all that because of what happened next? Or the other way around? The table was set for tea as usual when I came in, but I noticed that the napkins were laid on the chairs.

'What's this?' I said.

My mother waved a fist at me, pursing her lips, rolling her eyes to heaven—and in behind her, through the kitchen doorway, came a girl. I recognised her at once, even with her hair tied back, even in the long overall apron she wore—just unwrapped I could tell from the foldmarks. It was John Edward's cousin, Hannah, and she was going to be our new maid.

8

Our new classroom was upstairs—an old drawing room: tall windows on one side, a white marble chimney-piece on the other, a rickety glass-panelled door at the back, leading to a conservatory. On warm days the door was left open and a scent of flowers came up the aisles between our desks. One day a stray dog came in, hesitating until Father Rowan called him up to the rostrum where he curled nose to tail for the rest of History class. Through the windows, through trees, we could see rooftops, wave after wave of blue bangor breaking about this green island like a sea making for some far distant shore.

The New Hall: the words wove through everything those next few years like the builders' noise and dust. Besides the ring of trees around the grounds, there was a grove like a diameter between the schoolhouse and the priests' house. It was coming down, Father O'Conor announced one morning, to make way for a new hall. The two old houses were identical, though it was only when the trees were down that I noticed; then they looked as odd as twins side by side. They had been built by a Quaker family, Father O'Conor said; two brothers, he thought. He said he thought they had made money in coffee.

I imagined them coming home from coffee in the evening, chatting together up the avenue:

—I think thou shouldst give Murphy the sack.

—Was he rude to thee too?

—I could not repeat to thee the things that he hath said.

We were in Father Rowan's class a few days later when two men with a cross-cut disappeared into the grove. Half-an-hour later, Father Burke appeared with his camera and stood in the middle of the junior rugby field. The saw's hum stopped, we heard a shout, then a crack! and saw a towering ash tree tilt, rock back again, then slowly, silently heel over. Father Burke shaded the view-finder with his hand.

'The board, gentlemen!' Father Rowan was on his knees dashing more words into the bottom right-hand corner with a noise like a machine gun: ALPS SNOW PO ROME . . . crash!

The room became brighter as if a blind had been let up. Through the gap in the trees I could see Father Grenan on the croquet lawn winding on his camera. I think his was a Zeiss.

'And for your homework—look here, class is not over until I leave—I want you in your own words, using "I", to tell the story of Hannibal . . . . *I* was born in—in?—look it up . . . . My father was Hamilcar Barca, one of the most illustrious generals of captivity. *I* well remember the day, *I* was only nine years old, he took me into Spain and made me swear undying hostility to Rome . . . . Like that.'

Father Rowan gathered up his books, O Braonain ran to open the door for him, we ran to the windows to see the tree, still sinking to the ground as twigs and small branches gave way under the weight of the trunk with a crackling sound like sugar underfoot.

******

Those first years in our new house felt strange, like going up in a lift. We had not settled properly yet. One night my brother slept with me, the next with another brother, the next in a room by himself and the next we might all sleep together in one big bed.

It was strange too that across the road in Tranquilla Convent there was a corncrake, just as in Margaret's meadow.

'The fox must have brought him,' Hannah said when he finally stopped. She might even have been right-he never came back again. I pictured him, though, flying high above France and Spain on his way back to Africa where, according to *British Birds*, he spent the rest of the year—like Hannibal.

'I was born in . . . .'

A cold breeze blew down the back of my neck. That fly window I had once climbed in was still open, open because it was broken, I had found out. The bare room I had landed in had become the breakfast room, where we had dinner and tea as well. It grew dark. The apple trees faded and our reflections appeared in the long window barred with streaks of condensation.

'A newspaper, Adrian.'

'What?'

'. . . and six—is twenty-five . . . thirty-five—is fifteen—is one—four—nine—eleven—twenty-four. Twenty-four fifteen.' My father looked up from his ledgers. *'You are driving the pen into the mahogany table.'* He ruled a line with his red pen, reached for the blue.

'Anraith an giorria, feoil an coinín'. My mother passed me the *Press* to lay under my writing-paper. 'I . . . .'

'. . . thirty-six—is sixteen—is one—two—four . . . .'

'. . . used to hear my father saying.'

'Tell us,' Hannah turned to me, 'how do you spell "sand"?'

'Sand?'

My mother raised her hands to me behind Hannah's head, miming strangulation.

'S.a.n.d.'

'And I was thinking that.' She blushed. She held the pen so tight her fingers were white.

Silence again except for the clock and the murmur of figures from the head of the table.

Sand . . . . She was writing home. Sand . . . . That was why Brod's father had built the big new entrance with the cement

83

crosses on the piers: not into his land, vanishing slowly behind trees like Tranquilla Convent, but to let lorries in to the fish back hill, already a huge silver scoop twice the height of the house, that you could walk up right to the clayey band about the top where the martins had made holes for their nests, an arm's length in and teeming with big soft blue lice . . . .

'Have you nothing to do, Adrian? Is six . . . eleven . . . nineteen . . . and seven—is one . . . . Hannah, could you put on the cocoa, like a good girl?'

The brown square of parquet-patterned lino, the pine chest of drawers, the big Sacred Heart picture and another of the Holy Ghost hovering above the Holy Family: so much from our old house fitted into one room here. We lived in this warm room in the back—the damper out, the fire burning loudly—wild west settlers safe in the waggon circle of family. Some evenings I was so happy I got pins and needles in my fingertips. Sometimes we heard later that someone had called at the front door and had got no reply. Probably when my brother was doing his imitations of our new neighbours, when we were having our cocoa, when my father had finished his books and next morning's porridge was pop-popping in the kitchen. The bell-board was in the kitchen—we were cut off from the world once the cross door was shut.

'And taking the cup—he broke it . . . .' Hannah bounced in with the tray, adding soberly as my father glanced up, 'as poor Father Dillon used to say. Now, do the old fellow on the bike.'

My brother pulled up his grey stockings over the ends of his trousers and they were plus fours. Slowly he threw out a shaking leg, and he was Mr Clarke getting on his high bicycle and pedalling slowly down Palmerstown Gardens, looking over hedges into gardens. Such strange neighbours we had: women who wore sunglasses and drove cars, people who pronounced 'room' 'rum'.

'By the way,' my mother turned to my father, 'who's that

took old Deeney's shop?'

'Don't know, don't know.'

'They have it nice, mind you. What's this they called it—"The Irish . . . ."?'

'Well, if it's got "Irish" in it, you can be sure they're Jews.'

'Now,' my mother said, 'Our Lord was a Jew.'

'I—' Hannah blushed once more '—often heard that said.'

'Kkkmm!' My father cleared his throat. 'I'm not, thank God.'

'Who's this?' My brother got down on one knee, puffed out his nose and, shading gazing eyes with one hand, scribbled furiously with the other.

That was easy. That was—

'Mr Citron—'

'Oh, a good Cork name' my father put in.

—Taking down the number of the 12 bus that had not stopped for him.

'Mrs Citron was talking to me at the bus stop the other day,' my mother went on and she's a very umble woman.'

'It's humble.'

'Well—Kkkmm! I was in with Cohen today . . . .'

My mother winked at Hannah, who began to laugh.

That was the time, when my father was about to tell a story, that Uncle Paul, my mother's brother, always seemed to arrive. If we did have a visitor those evenings, it was Paul, hard evidence that not everybody lived in a family.

'Sssh!' Hannah was the first to hear him always.

'It's only the dog. Go on, Dada!'

'Sssh!' Hannah insisted, and then we all heard the dragging in of the heavy bicycle to the side-passage. Silence, then the tap of the steel bicycle clips on the window and we turned and saw Paul's face pressed up like a white mask against the glass.

'Kkkmm!'

I let him in through the conservatory. He waited always until he was in the breakfast room before he took off the black beret, pulled down all around like a helmet.

'No post?' No greeting ever. He sat down at once, catching his right trouser crease between finger and thumb and, shooting the leg out straight, tucked the other out of sight under the chair so he seemed to have just the one leg. He glanced up at the Sacred Heart lamp.

'Only the *Good Counsel* '. My mother took down the big brown envelope from behind the red lamp, glancing at the crossed-out address. 'I . . .' she faltered as Paul turned full around to face her—he had the slightest cast in his eye—'. . . see you were staying in Harold's Cross.'

'That crackpot.'

That (though it was some years since he had returned from living in London) was really all I knew about Paul: that he seemed to have rows with landladies and to change lodgings. He packed the envelope in his pocket, took out a large packet of Gold Flake and, in a minute, the room was filled with the unfamiliar smell of tobacco smoke, wreathing everywhere.

'Well, Paul, and how's everything?' My father smiled.

'Thp!' Paul spat out an invisible shred of tobacco. No small talk either. 'Nice shop that, Connolly opened up beside you. Nice shoes.'

'Is that so?'

'Just looking in there today. Ah yes, some nice stuff he has.'

Rrrr! My father put a little finger in his ear and gave it a ringing cleaning.

Paul turned to Hannah next. 'And how do you like living in Dublin?'

'Are you living around here now? Didn't I—' she smiled, she was quick like that. '—see you out at the shops there the other evening?'

'And you're from Ballyhaunis?' Paul drew down another deep lungful of smoke. 'What part?'

'Sure, you must know all that country?'

'Do you know any Foodys up that way?'

'Do you know the Foodys?'

Rrrr! My father cleaned his other ear.

Paul turned to my mother. 'You're not making tea by any chance?'

'Why didn't you say?' Mama made for the kitchen but Hannah beat her to it.

'Nice cut of a girl.' Seat stiff in the chair, Paul leaned a yard to one side, stretched his arm another yard and toppled ash a third yard into the fire. 'What's this her name is? Eileen?'

'On the way to Ballintubber, Eileen met a cattle jobber!' Mama laughed frantically loud, miming with her mouth— HANNAH.

'*Hannah.* Hannah what?'

'Dadda, didn't you want to hear the news?' TARPEY.

'*Tarpey . . . Tarpey.* The only Tarpey I . . . .'

The radiogram crashed into life and Paul sat back in silence, tilting back his flushed and furrowed forehead as he looked at the ceiling, taking off his wristwatch and rubbing his strong black-haired wrist. 'A bit too much of the BBC about that fellow.' He spoke aloud to himself.

'Do you like the sugar?' Hannah called in.

'You can bring in the sugar bowl,' my father murmured. '*The sugar bowl.*'

'No word from home?' My mother finished a darn, scuffing it with the backs of her fingers until it blurred into the rest.

'Yes. Dropped down there the other day.' Paul spoke as if Galway was around the corner. 'No. No news.' He sipped his tea steadily. 'And that's the only post?'

'That's all.'

'Thp!'

We sat in silence then until he stood up, pulled the beret down all around again, furled his trouser end and clipped it in place.

'I'll be in again.' He stood on the other leg and clipped again. 'I'll let myself out.'

'Kkkmm!'

I went with him through the dark to where he had left his bike, generally on the flowerbed outside the conservatory door, leading the way then round the house onto the road.

'Ought to get that down'—he nodded at our roadside chestnut tree—'blocking the light.' He put on his dynamo, lifted the back wheel, pedalled to see that it shone, sat into the saddle. 'What galls me'—he shifted up and down in the saddle until he was totally comfortable—'what really galls me about the postal system here is that you have no come-back. None.' He pressed a black toe against the kerb, pushing far out into the road like a boat onto a river, turning to call 'Night!'

Inside, my mother had somehow got my father to continue his story, hissing 'Sssh!' as I returned.

'. . . And this chap came in with a piece of silver—and a nice piece it was too.' He described a small circle in the smokey air. 'A Dublin chap, and he said "Would you be interested in this?" So there's old Cohen up at the counter, munching away at a big pickle sandwich—'

'Eeaugh! My mother threw up a hand.

'Didn't even look around. And the chap says "To tell you the God's honest truth" he says "I'm a bit stuck at the moment. What'll you give me?"'

My father imitated Mr Cohen's voice just right—'"Try someone down the Quays . . . ." And the chap says—"Look, just give me *something.* "' My father put a hand in his pocket, threw

88

it open on the table— "There's five bob if you want to take it," Cohen says. Two perishing half-crowns . . . . And he took it. *He took it*, and, when he went out the door, Cohen looked at me and winked,'—my father winked '—as much as to say . . . .'

'The hound!' Hannah said.

'You scrape down low enough, you'll see what they're made of. Ruthless. With a capital R.' My father rose and took the supper tray out to the kitchen, repeating to himself as he rinsed the cups, 'Yes indeed, with a capital R—' He took the Jeyes fluid from under the sink, went out, scattered some down the side-passage shore. '—With a capital R, sir.' He scrubbed his hands noisily and came back into the breakfast room, pulled out all the plugs except the Sacred Heart lamp's, glanced around the room. 'A capital R, he says . . . .' He took *The Irish Press*, folded it, stepped to the window and smote a bluebottle with such sudden force it spattered across the glass.

Clang-a-lang! Across the road, Tranquilla Convent bell rang as loud as if it hung on our chimney stack.

'O look where the moon is already!' My mother rose and shook out the *Press*, rolling the sheets into rods, tying the rods into wreaths all ready for the morning fire.

'Time for beebo!' my father smiled at me.

Sometimes, after a visit like that from outside, we were unsettled for hours, my parents' bed creaking as they lay awake.

When we finally settled on bedrooms of our own, mine was at the front. At night, as I lay waiting to fall asleep, if I heard a dynamo go whirring past outside, I wondered sometimes if it was Paul and where he was staying now, following him in my mind's eye down road after road of curtained houses, dark only for the moonlight glistening on the slates.

9

Saturday. My father's busy day.

Crack! Hannah put his shaving-water saucepan on the stair-post.

'Godgy-wodgy!' He went to the bathroom blowing against the morning cold. He was in good form . . . . 'Against the side!' He murmured a shout down the landing. 'Direct it against the *side* of the bowl.'

My brother heeled the toilet door shut.

'I think it should stay dry.' Crack! My mother struck a match, lighting a candle for autumn shoe weather.

Cocks were crowing in the yard of Fortfield House. That was the house in whose orchard our house had been built. When their land was sold, the people there, two silent Protestant sisters, must have withdrawn with every living thing behind that high wall. Their horse neighed. It reminded me of Noah's Ark.

'Are you up?'

'I—'

'You'll be handling a cold shovel—that's how you'll end up. If you don't smarten up.'

From my window as I dressed I could see the high wall topped with broken purple glass and a broken stone coat of arms. One Miss Stewart—I couldn't tell one from the other— was feeding the cats. Under a unicorn without a horn was a door. When I kicked it the dogs went wild.

God! I was meant to be serving Mass.

The convent bell clanged. Five to!

Three to. I was on my bike. The road ran straight down a

tunnel of trees from our front gate to the school back gate. One to. I skimmed past Father Rowan kneeling, eyes shut, in a frost white corner of the croquet lawn. I ran up the big steps, skated down the hall, into the back hall, to the notice board.

Blessed John Berchmans—Fr Rector: A. Gorman. A. Kenny.

The grandfather clock struck eight. A scent of fresh ground coffee came up the basement stairs. I ran up the main stairs and saw Father O'Conor at the end of the corridor. He had only got as far as the stole—dark gold this morning as the larch tree tresses waving outside the venetian window. I walked and got back my breath. Through a left-open door I saw an unmade bed like my own. Other little rooms had been converted to chapels. Berchmans was tiny. I squeezed between the altar and the wall to light the candles. I moved the chrysanthemums back from the flames, poured the wine and lit the stove.

Gorman slipped in, hands joined, but I could see the bicycle chain grease on his fingers. He whispered something to me but I pretended not to hear—to make him whisper louder, which he did, and Father O'Conor turned and stared at him. Sometimes I liked doing things like that to Gorman.

So it was not until Mass was over that I heard that O Braonain was leaving.

'Get lost. Where?'

'It's boarding. Somewhere down the country. They're Benedictines. His uncle's a monk there.'

'Monk!'

Uncle Paul knew all about it, of course. He'd met someone from there on a pilgrimage in Fatima or Lourdes. 'Or was it Rome . . . ?' He furrowed up his forehead.

'Not Knock?' Hannah said.

'No . . . no. I remember we had a glass of wine together.

Lisieux? It's on the tip of my tongue. An interesting man he was too. I remember one thing. He felt the same about Padre Pio as I do. A saint. But very abrupt. Very'

O Braonain left suddenly. It seemed to happen overnight, in the same strange way houses on Palmerstown Road suddenly turned into flats. One morning there was an old maid putting out an old bin, the next there was a row of shining new bins and a queue of girls with country accents at the bus stop.

'That's a good sign,' Mr Corcoran said when the O'Haras moved in. They had bought Dr Muldowney's—Ear, Nose and Throat—big red house just around the corner from us. Or was he Chest?

O'Hara was in my class but I hardly knew him. He sat at the back always, in the darkest corner, playing games he invented for himself. The latest was seeing how many parallel lines he could rule on a sheet of paper without their touching. He could draw them so fine and close together that unless you held it close it seemed to be a sheet of black. He never seemed to pay attention but always knew what was going on, I noticed. So did Father Wilmot one day he began explaining something to him.

'You needn't bother,' O'Hara interrupted politely.

We all waited for the rebuke, but it did not come. Father Wilmot looked at O'Hara as politely as O'Hara looked at him—and then *smiled*.

But so did I—a wet day Gorman and I were playing table-tennis, when I discovered he had no back hand (I was always discovering new sides to Gorman's clumsiness) and so I began returning the ball to that corner, until O'Hara, who was watching, said in his frightening, polite voice, 'Why do you do that? You know that he can't hit the ball there?'

Afterwards—I lost—O'Hara asked us both to his house.

They were still moving in. Everything had the right-wrong look of things that had been owned for a long time. It was different from home, different from Gorman's too. There was less of everything, everything seemed lighter—like the old framed British Rail poster a man was hanging on the wall—like Mrs O'Hara standing tip-toe beside him, saying 'I've had that since it was a postcard!'

The top floor was empty except for heaps of books. We were mooching up there one day when O'Hara's brother called up something to him from the landing below—I forget what but suddenly O'Hara was in a white rage, snatching up handfuls of books, screaming as he flung them down at his brother, who stood smiling until one struck him on the heel, when he shrugged and walked downstairs. That was the only time I ever saw O'Hara lose his temper.

He was tall and thin. You could almost see him growing, or at least see more and more of his black socks appear under the turn-ups of his new long trousers. Maybe that was what made his memory seem amazing. He remembered everything, right back to when he was baby. He told once, as we cycled home from school, what it had felt like to sit in a basin of warm water in the sunlight.

'Penrhyn' . . . 'Roseneath' . . . We free-wheeled down the footbridge . . . . 'Kimberley' . . . 'Kingston' . . . .

Protestant houses were easy to tell: they had hedges in front, their front doors were faded dark. They were like the black squares in a crossword.

'What are you doing today?'

'Do you want to come up to my place?' Gorman said.

O'Hara said 'Or mine?'

We were at Palmerston Road deciding when I saw my

Uncle Paul come pedalling along, looking straight ahead as always, carefully parallel to the old tram-tracks. I was going to call out when his arm went out and he turned into Cowper Road, so I pointed instead. 'My uncle. No one knows where he lives.'

'Let's follow him then,' O'Hara said. I had never thought of that.

A double decker went by. When it had passed, Paul was well up the road, pedalling steadily two feet out from the kerb.

'Inisfree' . . . 'Thorndale' . . . Past my house and up to the Rathmines Road. When we got there, Paul had vanished. We raced to the corner of Frankfort Avenue and glimpsed him around the bend. We raced again, catching up just as his arm swung out again and he veered right, looking over his shoulder and seeing us. He continued pulling across the road until his right foot was on the kerb, his head swinging left as we drew alongside. I waved, coasting on past, but O'Hara and Gorman had stopped at his 'Well well.' I doubled back.

'And who are these two men?'

While I introduced him, he took the bike by saddle and crossbar, plucked it vertically and lowered it onto the path, took off the beret, tucking it into the bulging green canvas saddle bag. He looked at his watch.

'Would you like to come in?'

I was amazed. So he lived here . . . only a few hundred yards from us . . . right under our noses. The front garden stank of cats and was wild. My uncle plucked the bike again, holding it aloft and showing those swarthy black-haired wrists, and lead the way down damp basement steps.

'There's a Teddy Boy element going round,' he said, wheeling the bicycle inside. He must have wheeled it the depth of the house. Gorman had time to say 'What does he do?', I to say, 'Don't know' and O'Hara to point out a heap of twigs in the area before he returned and showed us inside. There was a smell of must.

My uncle set a match to more twigs in the grate, shielded the match and lit the gas under a scrubbed shining kettle. '*Marbh le tae 's marbh gan é!*' He walked back to the fire with the match and, when O'Hara smiled, said something else in Irish. Soon they were chattering away, Uncle Paul standing directly in front of O'Hara, his blocky black shoes planted a good yard apart. He repaired them himself, I guessed as I noticed a last and what looked like a piece of old car tyre in a corner. As if my looks showed up, or even caused, some untidiness, Paul moved about the room shifting the matchbox an inch to one side, returning then to O'Hara. Gorman took up an *Independent* from a chair and began to read—the latest on Lunik 2, which had just struck the moon.

'*Agus, inis dom, cad a dheineann do athair . . . .?*'

Still speaking in Irish, Uncle Paul had got down to quizzing O'Hara. I went over to the window, looking out through rusting bars up at the garden. I half-expected to see hens rooting up in the long grass. The scent of burning twigs, the steam from the kettle wreathing about in the half-light, the beat of the big alarm-clock: it reminded me of the country. On the table was a blue check oilcloth and an open exercise book covered with Paul's neat blue handwriting. I turned, pretending to be interested in O'Hara's replies: as good at Irish as at everything else, he was describing his father's job—'the last sinecure in the Four Courts' he had told me.

'*Breitheamh,*' Paul hummed.'*Ar ndoigh! Agus, inis dom—*'
'*Saghas breitheamh,*' O'Hara interrupted politely.
I turned back and looked at the copybook:

Deus—a sincere friend
Notre Dame—
Where is your pride?

Passion of Christ, strengthen me as <u>I fight my way.</u>
Beware of too much religion: have interest, hobbies.
No split personality. Schizophrenia.
S-- What makes a man, what makes a woman . . . .

Suddenly, Paul was behind me, silent on his home-made
rubber soles. I heard him just in time and casually lifted a saucer
upside down on another saucer and looked at a cold fried rasher
there. He shut the copybook, put the saucer back on the saucer.
Dusting fingertips clean with his thumb, he said, 'Now, who'd
like a biscuit?' He put the copybook on a shelf and took down
a tin box; like almost everything else in the flat, it seemed to be
home-made. 'We have Mikado and Polo.' He looked at me
carefully but I just said, 'Can I have both?' and he laughed.

I had never seen him in such good humour. He fussed
about us with the teapot and biscuit tin, went over to the hearth
to brush fallen ash into the grate with what looked to be a hen's
wing. He settled finally, tucking one leg under his chair, shot out
the other, lit his cigarette and began firing more questions as he
spat out invisible shreds of tobacco.

'And Thp! what about you? Would you like to be a judge
too? Thp!'

To my surprise, O'Hara's face coloured and he said, 'I'd like
to be an artist.'

'An artist!'

'You mean a painter?' I said.

'Yes.' O'Hara fingered his dark-downed upper lip.

'That's a good one!' Uncle Paul laughed, a strange, high,
almost musical sound. 'That's a good one!' And, turning to me,
talking to me as if I was a stranger, he said, 'Thp! And yourself?
Off down the west again next summer, I suppose?'

'I suppose.'

'What's this your uncle's name is? We met once.'

'Petie?'

'And he still lives alone?'

'Still.'

'You need discipline to live alone.' He pronounced it di-sup-line.

O'Hara looked about the bare room and smiled.

'And Thp!' Paul had turned to Gorman. 'What does your father do?'

Gorman told him in one sentence, then said, 'What do you work at, Mr MacNicholas?'

For a moment, Uncle Paul looked as if he had been hit between the eyes. Then—'The newspaper business. The *Independent*. In plain English, canvassing advertisements.' Recovering, he began talking about himself. I was even more surprised when he got up, went to a chest of drawers and took out a bundle of those *Good Counsel* magazines, sometimes re-addressed to our house. He opened one, passed it to Gorman, and there was his name above an article.

'A Unique Newspaper,' Gorman read aloud and, to show interest, O'Hara and I each held it by a corner and leant over to read: 'In your wildest dreams can you ever imagine a time will come when our daily Irish newspaper will cater not merely for the mental requirements of readers, but have a balm to offer for *bruised* bodies and *aching* hearts as well? To prophesy such a change at present would, I am sure, subject a person to an endless amount of ridicule.

Still, it is a reality in at least one South American city at present and the city is none other than that great Argentine port, Buenos Aires. It possesses the greatest and unique newspaper in the world. Just listen to what it has to offer beside its daily Chronicle of Events. It maintains a staff of dentists and doctors for the poor, a free legal department, a public library, a free forum, a museum . . . .'

'Have you been there?' Gorman looked up, letting go the magazine at the moment O'Hara and I let it go. Uncle Paul made to catch it, missed it and, blushing deepest red, bent to pick it up.

We sat for a few minutes in silence then until Gorman's eye drifted to a bookcase and Paul, nipping trouser crease between finger and thumb, went down suddenly on one knee, genuflecting—I thought in panic—to a statue of the Child of Prague standing on top, in fact drawing out a handful of books which he passed about as he had the biscuits.

'Faber and Faber. Did some work for them during the war. Proof-reading, that sort of stuff.' More minutes passed as he described sitting up in bed correcting spelling mistakes by the light of the Blitz. 'What's this?' He opened a book, holding it at arm's length to read the title. It was getting dusk. '*Poems*. T.S. Eliot. Did you ever hear of him? He was famous. He signed that for me ... see. I remember he had a photo of the Holy Father behind his desk; it just goes to show ....' He turned another spine to the brown sunlight slanting down through the barred window. '*Poems*. Louis MacNeice .... He made a right mess of his life, I believe, poor chap ....'

He packed the books all back into a shelf, saying as if speaking to himself, 'Have you ever noticed that these fellows never really *tell* you anything? I've noticed that. You think they're going to tell you something. And they don't.' He dusted fingers on thumb, sat down again. 'Of course, my real job was on *The Universe*.'

'What?' I was panicking again.

'The Catholic newspaper,' he said shortly.

It seemed like ages until the six o'clock Angelus rang, loud and clear, from Rathgar Church, when my uncle stood up at once. 'Well, well. That was very nice.'

'Thanks for everything, Mr MacNicholas,' Gorman said, O'Hara too. I turned at the gate to wave, but Paul was blessing himself and, as we got on to our bikes, genuflecting, vanishing down into the area where he kept his kindling.

'Holy Smoke!' O'Hara said as we cycled home.

******

Was it my uncle I was imitating for Hannah that evening? Or someone else some other evening? In any case, it was the evening the Corcorans came to our house for supper and Hannah had us to herself.

'Adrian's *sly*. '

'Why?'

'It's the one thing I can't stand is a jeer, a common low jeer.'

'I was only joking.'

'Of course, it's true for them; they say anyone with ginger hair is the same.'

'It's auburn.'

'Arra—what are you? You're only a little giddimaun.'

I watched the cocoa steam swirl up into the dark beyond the light. My brother stirred his cocoa with the end of his pen, sucked it, dipped the nib in the bottle and stared at Father Hillery's question once again: A man carpets a floor four yards by four, leaving a border three feet . . . . 'Hannah, do you know how to do this? He drew up his legs and sat on them; drew a floor on his blotter.

'No more than Guard Finegan—' She leaned over him, her breast brushing his cheek, straightened again '—I'd have been a sergeant only I forgot to carry the one!'

My brother drew another floor on his blotter. A tear dropped and soaked into it and he dropped a spit to pretend the first drop was also a spit. If only you did not have to swallow. That was the snag in crying. I looked at the second hand of my watch . . . 10 . . . 20 . . . 30 . . . 40 . . . A grinding swallow.

'Throw it away to hell!' Hannah said.

'Ask.' I went over to look through the keyhole.

'Who?'

Mr Corcoran was looking around the dining-room as he ate, slowly. Mrs Corcoran was not. My mother was holding onto the seat of her chair as if she was in an aeroplane.

'That's a nice picture rail,' Mr Corcoran said finally.

'Ask Corcoran,' I said.

'The very thing,' Hannah said. 'Mind out of the way, you.'

And now I felt her breast as she pressed me aside, pressed an eye to the keyhole. The Corcorans, they were at school with us, had moved to a new house across the road. Mr Corcoran had built it. He was building the new school hall too. As soon as the trees had gone and the bulldozers tumbled out the stumps and levelled the mud, a big sign had gone up on stilts: CORCORAN.

My brother's shoes clapped down the side-passage, away into the dark. Hannah wore the same kind. She stepped out of them, see-sawing barefoot on the hearth, scratching the back of her head on the Sacred Heart lamp stand. 'I'm going having a bath. That fella'll be back there all night.' That was true. Corcoran's was a palace, with marble floors and a moat with goldfish. None of us ever wanted to leave it. I tried to keep the chat going, describing Corcoran's house but Hannah just yawned and went upstairs.

I looked through the keyhole again. My mother took a hand glistening from the side of her chair and drew it along the hanging folds of the tablecloth, our best tablecloth from her old home: old flour sacks ripped, bleached, stitched together and embroidered all over with tiny bright hard flowers; rucking up now as Mr Corcoran leaned across the table. Under the table I could see the gleaming yellow leather sole of one of his shoes, square-toed, nigger-suede brogues. From a leather case he took a stout cigar and struck a match. It went out. He lit another and let that burn out too. He was talking. The doors to the sitting room were open, making one big echoing room.

'In my book, there's the teacher—he looks after the mind . . . .'

'The mind,' Mama nodded.

'. . . and the doctor—he looks after the body . . . .'

'Ah yes, the body.'

'. . .but, first and last,' Mr Corcoran said, in such a serious voice Mama did not say anything at all '—there's the priest—' He struck another match and this time lit the cigar and drew on it until the tip was glowing. '—he looks after the soul.'

Through the keyhole, I could smell the strange rich smoke. He blew a smoke ring, glanced as it floated wobbling across the room.

'What's all this about a "Vatican Council"?' Mrs Corcoran said. She was smoking a slim cigar.

'That's what I don't know!' My mother spoke again in a strangely high voice.

SSSSHHHHH!

The water crashed overhead like a cloudburst, Hannah loved baths. They hadn't one at home. They didn't even have an Elsan.

Clang-a-lang!

Across the road, the Tranquilla Convent bell rang. Five to nine. I pictured the nuns getting out of warm beds, going downstairs in the cold dark. They were Carmelites, enclosed for life. 'Discalced Carmelites,' Uncle Paul said, said they followed 'The Primitive Rule'. At night, at dawn, no matter what time I woke, if I lay awake long enough I heard their bell ring and saw their chapel lights appear just above the swaying shadows of the boundary trees, like a ship on a dark ocean.

Sssshhhhwwwssshhh!

Hannah was making waves now; the water was sluicing up and down between her .... Through the kitchen, into the hall, past the dining-room—they were all talking now. From next door, the Protestant side, came a serious BBC voice and then the crackle of uproarious laughter. No sound from the bathroom. I went quietly upstairs.

There was a roar. The bath water running out and then, in the attic, loud as the door knocker, the rat-tat-tat of an airlock. She was running the wash-hand basin tap ... she was washing her hair.

Click.

She was unlocking the door.

Pit-tit-tit.

Running down the corridor to her room.

Pit-tit-tit.

And back again.

No click.

She was in her pyjamas standing in the doorway roughly drying her hair.

'Would you ever hand us out my comb like a good ladeen.'

Her room smelled of old sweat and sweet perfume. For coming in here and taking half-a-crown, my brother had been flogged until he could not cry. Well ... hardly.

'Where is it?'

'Is it not in the locker?'

Her Sunday shoes . . . dictionary—she was going to evening classes now ... exercise book—'The girl's typewriter' 'The girls' typewriters' ....

'What's on you!'

'Coming!'

'Is that other lad not back yet?'

'Nope.' I drew a finger-wide path along the big steamed-up mirror as I dawdled, wandered into the cubbyhole behind—

full of cardboard crates: Jeyes, Angiers, Glaxo and the olive oil my father heated and rubbed into my hair.

'Hi! Take care would he be knocking and us not to hear . .' She was bending forwards, combing her hair down in a water-fall before her face. There was no top button to her jacket, no—oh thank God—no Miraculous Medal pin either. It was like looking into a cave. My knees turned to water. I could see her breasts, still glowing strawberry red as their nipples, and be-tween them down to her stomach, rucked up into little brown ridges. She straightened, shaking drops off the back of her comb.

'You missed a bit.'

'Where?'

I took a step forward, yawning as I touched a tip of her hair.

'But come here—' She bent forwards again. '—Will you ever forget the morning himself went back?'

I was so close now I could see the pale veins in her breasts quivering as she laughed. The Corcorans had asked my parents over for drinks one icy Sunday morning and my father had slipped on their drive, ruined his best suit, had to come home again.

'And wasn't he as well off? She's the stuck-up yoke . . . . Now, am I right?'

I was looking at a dark grain running down her stomach and out of sight when she paloed her hair with two sweeps of the comb and saw me. Her body vanished, quick as a trout. It had all taken a minute, it would never happen again, but for one instant, I had had a keyhole glimpse of another world. And to think that that world lived under our roof! Slowly, like blood oozing to a cut, her face went red. She said nothing.

She said people always told the truth in their sleep. Al-ways. A girl she knew in Ballyhaunis, who had worked in a shop, was asked questions one night by the boss' wife and told

103

everything. *EVERYTHING.*

Say I tried that?

-Hannah, do you like Adrian?

—Mmm Adrian, baby . . . .

—Will you meet him some night?

—Where? Where?

—In the garage. After the rosary.

I couldn't.

Say *she* tried that.

I lay awake listening for the creaky floorboard on the landing. All I heard was a sound like an army coming up the stairs.

'They're a very deceptive house,' Mr Corcoran said.

'Yes,' my father said, 'they're deep.'

The footsteps faded down the corridor.

'And there's this—' I heard my mother say, and the creak of the cubbyhole door —little . . . .'

'And a *lumber-room!* ' Mrs Corcoran cried.

That's what we called it after that, the lumber-room.

O'Hara liked having us, Gorman and me, in his house, downstairs in the kitchen. His parents lived in the library, even had their meals there at a little drop-leaf table pressed up against a bookcase. All their books were unpacked now, four walls of them from carpet to ceiling. It was like a counterweight to the lightness in the rest of the house. The chimney breast was covered with framed drawings and photos—Emmet, Casement with hooded eyes downcast, Collins laughing, clasping gauntleted hands together, O'Hara's grandfather, a cheerful-looking man in a bowler who had been something in the Free State; there was a bust of Arthur Griffith on the mantelpiece and, hanging from an old bell pull, a small green-nosed caricature of de Valera. Mr O'Hara could not stand him, giving him a smouldering look each time he drove the shovel into the coal scuttle. O'Hara could not stand the room. A row of books behind his chair was polished shining by the back of his head, from his habit of leaning to gaze at the ceiling as his parents talked. He told me once that there were thirty-two bunches of grapes and, I think, forty-two vines leaves on the ceiling frieze.

Down in the kitchen all was bare, like O'Hara's drawings. He had shown some to me since that day in Paul's flat. They looked like geometry to me.

'What modern artist do you like?' I had said. 'Annigoni?'— the only modern artist I had heard of: my mother had brought me to see his portrait of Pius XII in the Mansion House.

'I think the "o" is short, as in "rotten". No—Mondrian. And Klee maybe.'

In fact, O'Hara's kitchen was quite like Paul's flat, with the same bare walls and barred window, although the garden outside was trim, being mowed bare again today by Fry, Mr O'Hara's court crier.

'Ladders?' O'Hara went into the larder. That was something else he did—invent private language. 'Biscuits' had changed into 'Jacobs', then changed again. It was hard to keep up with O'Hara.

'Are you serious about that—being an artist?' Gorman said.

'Of course, I'm serious.' O'Hara put the kettle on the Aga. 'What about you—what are you going to do?'

'At university? That's ages away.'

'Not really.'

'History, I suppose.'

I was not too surprised. As long as I had known Gorman, when he had not been getting 'talkings' or spilling cups of tea into his father's lap, he had been reading History.

'And yourself?' O'Hara turned to me. 'Writing? Wilmot's always reading out your essays.'

I took a match from the kitchen box and picked biscuit crumbs from my teeth. It was true. I liked writing. But . . . . I was picking my nose with matchstick when I noticed O'Hara looking at me. I twirled it out and casually rubbed the side of my nose with it.

'That's unworthy of you,' he said.

'What?'

'That.'

'I was doing nothing.'

'There's no need to lie about it.' He smiled.

'About what?'

'You know.'

'I don't.'

'Then you don't.'

I felt my face turn as red as the match head. Gorman looked

at his hands. We sat in silence. O'Hara had habits too, some-times hawking up yellow rubbery little lumps he christened 'nougat' and held on his fingertips to examine in fascination.

'Look at you and your . . . .'

'But I don't *lie* about it,' O'Hara said, then as usual again he said, 'Would you like to hear my new record?'

'What's that?'

'Peter Grimes.'

'I'd better be going,' Gorman said.

Gorman could not stand music. O'Hara loved it. Upstairs in the big bare back drawing-room, he lay in an armchair and closed his eyes. I could not follow it but I liked day-dreaming to it, looking out of the french window at the afternoon clouds moving by. But not today. It was as if that match—it was still in my hand—had been struck and in its blaze I saw myself again picking my nose. And suddenly then, as if the blaze had grown, I saw Petie putting a finger to one nostril and shooting snot out of the other as he wandered over the hill. Then Austin's big clumsy hands appeared, tattooed with coal dust lodged under the skin . . . . and John Edward's rotten teeth and shaven head.

'. . . Peter Grimes! Peter Grimes! PETER GRIMES!'

I looked across at O'Hara. He was smiling, eyes shut as the harsh music rose. I had had this uneasy feeling before: that day in Paul's flat, when he had said 'di-sup-line' and O'Hara had smiled. I was not smiling now as I realised why I had thought of Petie, Austin and John Edward. It was as simple and clear as one of O'Hara's 4H pencil drawings. Because I was like them. It was like a bang on the head.

'What do you think? O'Hara had got up and was lifting the needle. Taking the record carefully by the edges between his palms, he looked at me.

I paused as if I had a great deal to say but then—lucky me! Mr O'Hara's deep Northern judge's voice called across the hall from the library, 'Jim! Would you take this tray downstairs for your mother.'

11

A bit of a blur then, as you'd expect after a bang on the head. What was I doing all those afternoons after school? Not playing rugby anyhow, in spite of The Morley Method of Scientific Height Improvement (3/9 post incl.): a bit of that blur is the messenger boy flying past in my green jersey; Father O'Conor had told my mother that she could give it away, provided the crest was removed. Not out with Gorman or O'Hara either: another bit of the blur is Gorman free-wheeling past on his way down to O'Hara's. A single clear picture, like the snipped-off rugby crest left on our breakfast room mantel piece, is Tranquilla Convent.

One afternoon, I went over to see if Corcoran was in. He was playing rugby, but I noticed that the convent boundary wall, Corcoran's garden wall, sloped down to a height you could climb—ten foot of granite, so full of mica it shone that day like a mirror in the sun. Soon I was going over to Corcoran's every day. An eight-foot drop and I was standing under the cypress wall. Through that, then over a barbed wire fence, under a paling, through a thorn hedge and I was inside.

Alone. A. Lone. Al. One. Alo. Ne. Alon. E. Alone.

A pigeon soared and clapped its wings—a sound like a gunshot. A magpie was standing on a donkey's back picking ticks, starlings running about its feet picking at the ground disturbed; for the grass was close matted. Strange fields in there, branches lying rotting where they had fallen, magpies drinking from the water-filled sockets in the trees.

When the bell rang, I ran. But I came back another time, and another. In, out, a hundred times, but like the crusty gold stitches in that rugby crest, they made a single picture.

Ten acres, Mr Corcoran said. He told me the nuns had been there for a hundred years. Ten acres was what Grandma had and I had crossed it in ten minutes. Here it would have taken me a hundred years, inching from tree to tree, wriggling on my belly. Everything stood out hugely clear: the salmon pink bark scales on the scots pine, the pigeons' breasts plumped out. Wood pigeons were everywhere, perched motionless, just above my head. I saw one in a nest of half-a-dozen twigs put her beak into her squab's beak and feed it a thick yellow cream, her eye all the time gazing down at me. Eyes everywhere. A butterfly, dowdy invisible, snapped open its wings and showed two glittering gold and purple marks like peacock's eyes. I heard a noise at my feet like a needle on glass and, looking down, saw screaming up at me a tiny whiskered creature. A pigmy shrew, I learned when I got home, from Arthur Mee's *Children's Enclycopaedia*.

It was as though I was seeing for the first time everything I had taken for granted in Grandma's. Wriggling through the grass—a scent so fresh I could feel it against the back of my chest as it went down—I went a little further each time: a ditch brimful of water . . . a row of graves . . . a bonfire sending up a pale rope of smoke. Beyond it was a wall as high, but over it came—'We'll prune back next year'—Mrs Jobling-Purser's voice from Rathmines Castle, where Mrs Corcoran had been to tea.

When I got home, my clothes were sparkling with cuckoo-spit, and the tiny pop-eyed creature in it: according to Arthur Mee, '. . . the frog-hopper or froth fly, which punctuates vegetation, turns the sap to frothy bubbles and lives in them as if in a castle . . . .'

Reasons for everything but, as Hannah said, currants for cakes.

******

A blackbird sitting on our gatepost flew singing up onto the lamp-post. I could see his throat ripple as he flew singing up into the chestnut tree I could see that he could not help singing.

'Who's that?'

'Me. Where's everyone?'

'Your Mam's gone out.'

'*Out!* Where?'

Mrs Gorman . . . Mrs Corcoran . . . sometimes they were in, sometimes they were out—organising jumble sales or . . . . I had never really thought about it. It had seemed as natural as my mother always being in. Without her, the house had the free unreal air of Christmas.

'She went to the pictures.' Even the air seemed clearer. Hannah's voice carried from the sitting-room like a shout. '*The King and I.*'

'What are you doing?'

'What do you think?' She flicked her duster at me. I flicked it out of her hand and she put her hands around my throat, pretending to choke me. This was the latest game. We wrestled silently about the room. One evening, upstairs, we really had nearly choked each other, had fallen back on a bed, red-and-blue-faced, not able to speak.

'And me with the whole house to do . . . .' She stepped back, tidying her hair. There were white scurfs of dried sweat on the armpits of her brown blouse. She dusted again . . . the Sèvres vase . . . the framed photo—present from Paul—of Padre Pio in his blood-stained mittens . . . the ivory Chinaman with the dead heron on his shoulder, walking along the mantelpiece to the precipice at the end he never reached . . . .

111

'Get out from under me, you!' She could be broody lately. She snapped her yellow rag at the bird on the ormolu clock that never worked.

On the nest of tables—*Time* magazine, still in its buff wrapper. Snf Snf . . . that foreign smell. My father had filled in a subscription form for three months. After four, it was still coming although he had written to Amsterdam to stop it. *The World . . . Science . . .* I turned the pages . . . *Theater.* My hands stopped as my eyes caught a photo of a great dark woman, face shining like coal, all naked but for a glittering belt and another fringe about breasts as big as—
'What're you hatching in here by the fire for?'
'Nothing.' My hands began to shake.
Belle of the Belly Dancers—The Bright Side of Nasser's Egypt. The caption cut off the photo at the knees, just below thighs bent straining back like Atlas, belly thrust forward, arms outstretched, face upwards. My breath went dry in my throat.
'I think I'll have a bath.'
'Do not. The boss'll want that water!'

'Weasel,' she called me. What would she call me now if she saw me—opening the hot press and putting on her fancy new brassiere, filling it out with my old rugby socks. Fierce Egyptian heat throbbed from the copper cylinder, wild oriental music too, as it refilled.
Shahshahshah . . . ratatata . . . bebeebeebebeebeeeeee. I swayed to the beat. *Belle* . . . that meant beauty. Beauty beauty beauty . . . vanishing away under wreaths of steam. The flushed face blurred to a mask again. I stepped to wipe the mirror clear . . . I felt a heavenly tremble . . . felt the floor shake.
Hannah! Coming down the corridor. I looked at the door. The unshot bolt looked at me like the barrel of a gun. I bolted

into the lumber room and hid behind the crates.

'Are you in there?'

I heard the bathroom door open, heard her turn off the tap.

'Where are you?'

The lumber room door creaked open, light poured down the floor. I crouched gazing at an old newspaper under my feet, the headline 'Fifteen Nations Meet for Air Talks' burned into my mind forever.

'Of course, he's such a peata....' Her footsteps faded down the corridor. I thought I heard her on the stairs and flew tiptoe down to my room, skidding to a stop when I heard her there.

'He's like a ....'

Like a fool I ran downstairs. She must have heard. From the dining room I heard her coming down and I ran into the conservatory. From there I heard my mother's key in the front door. I ran out into the back garden.

The day Mrs Corcoran had 'called', my mother hid behind the Pyrocanthus. But that had been in summer and she had had her clothes on, of course. My skin went as red as the berries, then blue as the Ceanothus. From there, I heard a rustle: the hedgehog Father O'Conor had given me from the school orchard looked at me with bright eyes.

If I was seen.

High above our garden rose the red brick battlements of Fortfield House. It would be just the day a Miss Stewart went up there to take the air ... gazing first across Tranquilla's fields to Rathmines Castle, turning slowly east then .... She would not say anything, of course, just slip a note in our letter box after dark, the way she slipped in the ground-rent notice. 'I will not brook naked boys ....'

The brassiere buckle pinched my back as I huddled down lower into the clay, full breasts resting on my knees. Through the bushes, I saw my mother come into the breakfast room, taking off her hat with the silly pheasant feather. And then—not raining now but pouring, spilling out of the heavens—Uncle Paul appeared. I sank still lower, watching through a crisscross tangle of twigs as he went to the window and stared out, eyes wide, lips moving. Bits of what he said carried out through that open fly window:

'And I could have—'

'But can't you . . . .' My mother went to the Sacred Heart lamp, took down a large brown envelope and handed it to him.

'Jesus!' And now Paul was flinging the envelope across the room, whirling about again to stare out at the garden.

'But what can I do . . . .' My mother approached him and he turned, screaming, 'You bitch!' He struck her across the face and rushed out of the room.

Slowly I rose on numb hunkers as my mother went down slowly on her knees on the hearth. Courage! Rising to my feet as she looked up at the Sacred Heart, opening her arms to it.

Now! I flew in giant strides to the conservatory door, saw the dining room empty ahead. Up the stairs, three at a time, handing off the stair post as I flew down the landing, hearing again Father Hillery's cry the day I actually scored a try—'By the Lord Harry! That was a nice one!'

****

Free-wheel, no hands, between the old tramtracks down Palmerston Road . . . past Mrs Yeats waiting for a 12 . . . one push on the pedals at Portobello . . . then free-wheel again all the way into town . . . bump bump bump down the cobblestones to Wellington Quay.

'Hello, Mr Reisenbach!'

'Zere y'are.'

'Any more books on butterflies, Mr Reisenbach?'

'Vet till I tell you. Ze missus got a butterfly in our flat z'other night. Janey Mac! It was as beeg . . . .'

'It might have been a moth. If it was night, Mr Reisenbach.'

'Zere y'are.' He went back to polishing a pewter eggcup and I glided over to the damp bundle of *Weekend* magazines that smelled of paraffin.

'Top fashion model Olivia normally takes a photograph session in her stride, but this time it was different. Olivia had yielded to persuasion and agreed to appear *au naturel* before the camera . . . .'

'Mr Reisenbach—'

'Vat?'

'How much is that print in the window? Of the Parthenon?'

'Zat's a *mezzotint* —' He reached painfully in to fetch it.

Until one day he glanced around and saw me shoving a centre page up under my jumper. He moved very quickly, coming between me and the door.

'Sure eet's no good if you are taking zem. Come here till I see vat you have.'

I stood still till he approached me, dodged around him, then out the door—and I was on my bike pumping the pedals across Capel Street bridge, letting the page fly on the Liffey wind, burning around the far quays, back across Kingsbridge and up into James Street, down Thomas Street, zig zag through Meath Street and into Francis Street where I risked a backward look. No sign of a black squad car, no sign of Mr Reisenbach's dirty blue yacht cap. I rested a foot on the kerb, my blood pumping hot. At the end of Francis Street rose the Dublin hills, the shape and colour of night clouds. I waited until safe blue dusk rolled down from them before I cycled home.

I had thought always that the streets ran out into the

country. Outside my father's shops on Sunday morning, while inside he went over Saturday's receipts again, I looked at the hills where we would be driving that afternoon:Three Rock, Tibradden and beyond. Now I saw that it was the other way round too. The country ran into the city. Capel Street, Parnell Street . . . every afternoon further . . . everyone was there: my father—I saw him once across O'Connell Bridge, looking grim, holding the brim of his hat. Uncle Paul too—a wet day in Abbey Street he sailed past on his bike, his hot-looking forehead uptilted to the downpour.

In fact, Uncle Paul above all; he seemed to be everywhere— out canvassing those adverts for the *Independent* I suppose. Down a lane behind Moore Street, lined with women chopping outer yellow leaves from cabbages with their knives: I do not think he saw them, let alone me, as he pedalled straight, looking ahead. One day I saw him wheeling his bike along a gutter, holding a piece of wastepaper in his hand, and followed him until he dropped it in a bin when he mounted his bike again. I saw but was not seen. Except once, a foggy evening I was cycling home (torn-out page inside my jacket) when I almost ran down Father Rowan standing at the head of a side street. He pointed down glistening cobbles to the yellow blob of a street lamp at the end and smiling, embarrassed, drew a camera from inside his old raincoat: 'I thought if I could just *capture* that . . . .'

******

A blackbird skimmed over the back garden wall and the next, the next, his evening screech rising and falling as if he was flying under arches.

'I'm doing my homework in here.'

'I'm not stopping you.' Hannah stuck a needle in the pincushion and tossed it onto the mantelpiece.

116

'Where's Mama?'

'Out.'

Out! Twice in the one month! 'Where?'

'She went to some Irish thing. She said she'd be back at ten.'

Ten!

'KKKmmm!' from the dining room.

'What's Dada doing?'

'He lit a fire in there. I thought you had homework?'

'Only memory work.'

She sat down at the fire with *Ireland's Own* and crossed her legs. I opened my book. 'So perished the French monarchy. Its dim origins stretched out and lost themselves in Rome. It had already learned to speak and recognised its own voice when the vaults of the Thermae echoed to the slow-footed steps of the Merovingian kings . . . .' She had her new shoes on, which my father had given her, with the baby Louis heels. The first day she wore them, she fell down the stairs. Her Kayser nylons too, that my mother had given her. I thought of that evening when Brod had tossed her can of paraffin and a lighted match across the road before Mannion's car and a burning drop had landed on her leg. 'Look up that vast valley of dead men crowned and you may see the gigantic figure of Charlemagne, his brows level and his long white beard tangled like an undergrowth, having in his left hand the globe and in his right the hilt of an unconquerable sword . . . .'

Her lips moved as she read an advertisement. From the table I could make out the top line — HAVE YOU A VOCATION? and other big words down the page — NURSING SISTERS LONDON GOD.

She looked up and I heard the hall door open. Mr Levidis' deep voice. Greek grind tonight. My brother had glasses now. He was sleep-walking too. One night he got up, went downstairs and opened the hall door, and then went back to bed. In the morning, the hall was full of leaves.

'Did I—' she turned to me '—tell you Daddy got a new job? Taking tolls.'

'What's that?'

'Well, supposing you sold a beast at the fair. Well, Daddy'd be on the road before you and you going home and he'd take toll from you. It's a shilling a cow, I think.'

'How would he know I sold a cow?'

'Wouldn't he see you?' She pokered the fire absently. 'Anyway, my brother does be along helping him.'

'Which one?'

'Haven't I only the one. Ownie.'

'You've four!'

'They're only stepbrothers.'

'How do you mean?'

'And you the scholar! Sure, my Mammy died when I was a baby. Daddy married again.'

'You never said that.'

Her face went a darker red. 'Oh her own children in by the fire. I was the one sent to town all weathers—and what I brought home I never got. Sure it wasn't home at all.'

'And was it long before he married?'

'Not long enough.' She drew out the glowing poker, laid it on the hearth. 'Not long enough.'

'Who used to mind you when you were small?'

'A girl used to come in.' She smiled. 'No more than myself.'

'What was she like?'

'Oh, a greasy yoke.'

Clang-a-lang! Tranquilla bell echoed down the chimney. She smiled again. 'Haven't they the hard life? In and out of bed like that.'

'I saw one the other day.'

'You did not! And did she see you?'

'I couldn't tell you.'

'That's a sin. What was she like?'

'She was the other side of the hedge.'

Hannah was laughing, so was I, when she said, 'Do you know what I saw one day?'

'What?'

'Remember the day your Mam went to the pictures?'

'With Uncle Paul.' I smiled. '*The King and I*.'

She didn't. 'And you said you were going to have a bath.'

Suddenly I felt my back turn ice cold. 'Did I?'

'You remember.' She looked at me.

I gazed, dazed, at the mantelpiece. My rugby crest was still there, a stiff embroidered shield, the Cross of Cong, which had been made for Father O'Conor's family. No use to me. I looked at her, and the face, that had seemed so ordinary a moment before, seemed suddenly like those dowdy Peacock butterflies when they opened their wings.

'Yes,' I heard myself whisper.

'And what did I see—' she lowered her voice '—only your Mam kneeling on the hearth there, praying. And do you know what she was saying?'

Oh thank God. 'What?

'"Dear Lord, take care of Paul" she said over and over. I wasn't listening now. I was in the kitchen and the cross door there was open, "Jesus look after Paul" she said.' Hannah lowered her voice still more. 'Sure, I don't think he's all there, do you?'

The fright was over, relief flooded in. I went and sat down beside her by the fire.

'Maybe they had a row.'

'Maybe.'

I crossed my legs, swung my toe. She swung hers, tapped mine. 'You've a neat little foot, mind you.'

'So have you.'

'Would you like a glass of milk?' She got up fussily and went to the kitchen. We had just got a fridge. 'Isn't it grand cold?' She sat down beside me again. 'Isn't it?'

Zzzzz. The big Bosch hummed—lest they see it, my mother locked the kitchen when old friends called—Zzzzz. We sat in silence as electrically loud. Out of nowhere came that thought again. I was like Hannah. She scratched an ankle with a heel. I did the same. The same. But now—like water suddenly buoying us up when we find we can float, if only for a moment—it was a beautiful thought. We were the same.

'Well.' She drained her glass and stood up. 'I'm going writing a letter home.'

Limply, I did the same. 'I'm going into the sitting room.'

'KKKmmm!'

He was doing a tot on the back of an envelope. 'Finished?' He sat up, shoved a hand down the front of his trousers and straightened himself. 'How are you finding it?'

'All right.'

He put the envelope in his pocket. *David Copperfield* lay open on his lap. The pages sprang up and slowly fell over . . . an illustration—Mr Wickfield pointing at Uriah Heep and crying, 'And now I finally see you for what you are! You!' On the blank back was another tot, the noughts strung like beads on his flying lines.

'I thought we might sit in here from now on. In the evening. What do you think?'

'I think so.'

Clup. He shut the book.

'Oh, Father Wilmot said we weren't to bother getting *Sard*

Harker. Remember you ordered it from Mr Hanna. He said it was vulgar.'

'Who's this that's by?'

'John Masefield.'

'You get people like that.'

'We're to get *Trent's last Case* instead.'

'Fair enough.'

He had his quiet voice, the one for business on the telephone. Funny how a hoarse half-whisper could sound so frightening.

'KKK-*mmm!*' That was better.

'Yes, you'll meet people like that. They seem attractive at first but, after a while, you'll notice that their friends' —he moved his hand to one side— 'slide away, they drift off; they leave your man on the corner. That's why they're called—'

'Corner boys.'

'Yes, they hang around there for some other fellow they can latch onto, tell a few smutty stories to—'

'Then he drifts off.'

'And then he drifts off. It's a sad sort of life. There's not much to that type . . . .' His toe swung like a pendulum.

'What do they look like?'

'Just a moment . . . . But you'd be surprised how easy it is to drift into that type of life. Very very easy. It's exciting you know, it's different. But you'll soon get tired of that; that's if you've any spark in you at all. And they don't like it when someone leaves, they don't like that, believe you me. But that's all right, that's their business . . . .' He looked at the fire. Gorman got a 'talking' as a punishment but, for me, this was a treat, as rare as my mother going out.

'Kkmmm! It starts with the little things. You might see a shilling on the mantelpiece and say to yourself, I might as well have it as the next fellow—'

121

'Yes.'

'*LEAVE IT.* It doesn't matter if there's an inch of dust on it. And if some other fellow comes along and puts it in his pocket—good luck to him. All you have to say to yourself is—Is it mine?'

'No.'

'Fine. Grand. That's all right. *WALK AWAY.* ' His hand walked out into the dark again. 'People aren't blind you know. You blot your copy and you'll see soon enough. You're marked down then, they're watching you then, and when you're down no one wants to know you—no one . . . .'

'Mr Kenny—' Hannah's head appeared round the door. 'I'm just going out to the shops for a moment.'

'That's all right, Hannah. And Hannah—'

'What's that, Mr Kenny?'

'You can sit in here whenever you like, you know.'

'Thanks, Mr Kenny.' Quickly she pulled the door shut again.

His toe, swinging an inch above the brown-veined hearth tiles, cracked down suddenly on the glowing crust of slack and it sprang up in flames. 'Now, did you have your supper?'

'No.'

'Would you like an egg flip?'

'O yes.'

He stood up, stood a fire-guard in the hearth. 'What do you think? I got it from Cohen.'

I looked at the hammered-out figures in thin pale brass, bustling about what looked like an ancient forge.

'I thought it had a nice Kkmmm! line.'

From upstairs I heard him rattling in the kitchen, flustered as when visitor called.

Cre-ek! He broke the shells off one another. A two egg flip tonight!

Teeth . . . pyjamas . . . prayers . . . Just-into-bed-in-time. His signet ring hot from the glass burnt my forehead as he stood stroking back my hair. With sheet for a glove, I held the glass and sipped the scalding yellow froth, with a queer, different taste tonight.

'I put drop of *spirits* in it . . . .' He hovered smiling by the bed.

******

'Quick!' It was a night not long after that I heard a door open. 'Oh quick!' I opened my eyes and saw my mother standing over me. It was morning really. Already a blackbird was singing outside. Hannah's door opened. We all went into the big bedroom. The light was on, my mother's eyes blinking against it. Their double bed was heavy, but my father's trembling made it rattle from head to foot. I was still half asleep and everything had the strange clarity things have sometimes when you get up in the night. The big picture of the Little Flower leaned out on its cord as if it would come crashing down. The candlewick curtains stirred in a dawn breeze, making a thousand different shapes.

'I'll get the Knock water!' my mother cried.

'I think it's under the sink!' Hannah called down over the bannister.

My father's teeth were chattering, his fingers rattling a rosary beads. The bed clothes were thrown back off his chest, heaving up and down as he gasped for air, which he sucked in between lips white with froth. My mother appeared with the holy water. It made no difference.

'Have you no drop of whiskey, Mrs Kenny?'

My mother looked at the Little Flower, then went downstairs, coming back with the visitors' bottle. It made no difference either. My father's eyes rolled white as he looked up at the

123

ceiling, panting.

'I'll ring Dr Gorman,' I said.

Their phone rang for just the same length of time it rang when I used to call Gorman. Dr Gorman sounded as if he had been up for hours. He said he would be with us in five minutes; in the meantime, we should raise the end of the bed. I got a four-volume life of Queen Victoria from the study and put two volumes under each end leg. My father seemed like a ghost.

Dr Gorman was shaved and brushed, his tie exactly knotted. He stood by the bed, looking down calmly as he took my father's pulse, took the stethoscope and listened to his heart, gazed into his eyes and then shook his head.

'There was many a man took up after the priest,' Hannah said.

Dr Gorman nodded, then said, 'No no, I think it was just a nightmare.' He looked down at my father and said it again in the same calm voice he had one day I overheard him give Gorman a 'talking'. 'Yes, I think it was a nightmare.'

Slowly, the rattling stopped, my father's hold on his rosary loosened. Dr Gorman looked at the whiskey on the locker and said, 'I think a good cup of tea . . . .' Hannah was downstairs before he had finished, my mother after her.

'A nightmare . . . .' Dr Gorman nodded again, feeling his small firm chin, then stood away from the bed, chatting with me.

'Well, we haven't seen you for quite a time now.'

'How's Anthony?'

'Thriving. Thriving.'

One night I was with them in their back garden, looking out for the Gagarin sputnik, when Gorman bent to tie his shoelace and, straightening suddenly in the dark, his head hit his father's chin full force. I had the same smothered skip of delight now as Dr Gorman went on: 'In fact, he was asking about you the other day, you and—who's that boy with rather a lot to say for

124

himself?'

'O'Hara?'

'Yes, he wants to have you both up to tea one of the evenings.'

My father was quite still by the time Hannah returned. He opened his eyes, murmuring to himself 'a nightmare.'

They showed Dr Gorman downstairs then but—I was sly (or was I thinking of that girl Hannah had told me about, who told everything in her sleep?)—I leaned over my father and whispered, 'What was it?'

'I . . . .' he whispered back, his hot breath making a small wreath of steam in the chill air, then shut his eyes and fell asleep. In the morning, he did not remember anything, he said.

I often wondered what it had been. Once, long after, I overheard him say, 'Starting a business without capital—*madness* . . . .' and I wondered if that had been it. But I never found out.

12

The long pale hand reached out, drawing like a telescope the frayed white cuff from the frayed black coatsleeve from the green-black gown. Gorman drew in his breath, as he did when he was in for a 'talking', looking left and right out of the corners of his eyes. The fingers passed over his shoulders.

'Adrian.'

I stood out of the line. Father O'Conor did not even look at me. I stood beside him, watching everyone else file down the courtyard steps into school. The last boy vanished.

'Yes, father?'

He turned and looked about him at a few remaining work-men feeding bits of planks and cement bags to a fire. The hall, its clocktower, library and staff room were finished, granite-walled, copper-roofed; and the corridors, granite arms embrac-ing the old houses. HIC LAPIS . . . . From where I stood I could read the foundation stone. The day it was laid Father O'Conor set a copper canister behind it and, as it was cemented down into place, explained that it held a scroll with the name of every boy in the school. The thought had thrilled me at the time; now I turned cold as a stone. He looked up at the tower, up at the clock, checked it with his watch. *I want perfection,* the blue eyes seemed to say. They raked across me and I followed him, down the courtyard steps, in the basement door, up the stairs past Father Williams' office—he was at the doorway, stooping to dab TCP on a boy's knee—it seemed beautiful as home. The smell faded. We were going up the main stairs. Down the stairs came the sound of Dominic, the handyman, practising the flute. He lived on the top floor, near Father O'Conor's office, where I had never been. Joss and Art had, and now they were gone.

Each step I remembered something. I had stolen a copy of *Men Only* in Charlotte Street, hidden it, stuck it in a cleft in a tree in Tranquilla Convent. *Oh My God.*

'Yes, father?'

Silence.

The music rose. We were going down a gloomy corridor and I realised suddenly that, even inside, the two houses were identical. I had walked down this corridor every morning in the other, priests', house when I had served Mass. The room at the end would be Berchmans— Father O'Conor was stopping at it now, unlocking the door. It was his office. I followed him inside and he shut the door. Without even looking at me, he said, 'Off with the jacket, down with the pants.'

I could not move. I was in for what Joss and Art called a turn-up. a bend over flogging.

'Quickly.' He put down his book. I gazed dumb, numb at the title, *Readers Digest Companion*. He placed his biretta on top of it.

'Why?'

'Were you cycling down the footbridge?'

'No.'

He caught me by the wrist and I broke into tears—cunning tears—and yet they came in a flood that amazed me more than shamed me.

'Oh, *now* . . . .' He let me go, then put his arms about me, taking me into his lap. I must have been heavier than he thought. He shifted his long legs apalo and settled in his chair. 'Now . . . don't cry.'

I went on crying as he took a bar of Aero chocolate from his pocket and slowly peeled off the silver paper.'Now, what's wrong?'

Why, with all I had to choose from, did I choose Paul? 'It's my uncle—' And as if I had been thinking of nothing else, I described Paul's accident. (He had been knocked off his bike by a car.) I had almost forgotten it, yet described it as if I had seen it.

'And is he all right now?'

'Yes.'

'You must be close to him?'

'Yes.'

He shut his eyes, shut for almost a minute—as if picturing Paul shooting off his bike, flying through the air, clipped trouser ends outspread like Hermes' winged ankles, beret-helmeted-head-first into Griffith's of Wicklow Street corner window. 'How well it was a shoe shop,' my father had said.

Ba-Ang! From far below, came the noise of workmen's sledgehammers. They were breaking a doorway from the schoolhouse into the new corridor.

Father O'Conor opened his eyes again, shifting his long legs again. 'And your mother?'

'She's grand.'

'And there's nothing else?'

'No.'

'You try to be good?'

'Yes.'

He put his arms about me and rocked me like a baby. In our history book there was a picture of one of his ancestors, fierce with a forked beard and a sword. I thought of that now, perhaps because the pale red circle his biretta had left about his forehead made me think of a crown. It was pressing gently against my head now. He had a black leather sheath on one of his fingers—he was always cutting himself pulling up weeds and briars—and he patted my knee with it. When Father Kiely held my hand, his face had a confused, excited flush that embarrassed me, but I felt at ease now. Through the window I could see the tips of a walnut tree dancing in the breeze. In the door came the sound of Dominic playing *Greensleeves*. I breathed in the dry scent of Father O'Conor's gown. I had always dreaded that I might be here someday, and now I was—and I was safe.

'Well, now.' He spoke again, shifting his long legs yet again. 'And tell me . . . Who is your best friend? Anthony? Jim?'

'Yes, father.'

'Good . . . and tell me, what books are you reading?'

I told him. 'Do *you* read much, father?'

He shook his head. 'Once I did, rather . . . .' But, instead of the books he had read, he told me about birds that had grown tame about him, one time he had been ill and used to sit in his garden at home.

I asked about the garden, but he told me about the house. Now it belonged to the Italian ambassador. I paid attention as his face turned cold as he described how they had driven nails into panelling to hang pictures.

The bell rang downstairs.

'By Jove!' as suddenly as he had caught my wrist, he let me go. He brushed down his gown skirts and tossed the silver paper he had rolled into a single ball into the wastepaper basket. I looked about the room, utterly bare but for a crucifix.

'Off with you!' He stood up smiling. 'And you weren't cycling down the footbridge?'

'I wasn't.'

I was I was I was I was I was . . . . I went downstairs and into class, wriggling with delight. Gorman caught my eye and his face split into his old smile. It was true for Hannah—I was a sly weasel. Still, it was a long time—Hannah had long gone to London—before I cycled down the footbridge again.

I remember her going as a series of clicks! like the click-clack! of the milkboy's bent-pedal bike that day she arrived.

Click! of the gate that night she came back from the shops. Shops, my eye. Sly boots slipping out to post a letter.

Click! of the letterflap not long after: a letter for her from London. A convent had accepted her.

Click! Click! Click! a few months later. We were in Mayo when she left, my brother and I. We called to her house on our way home from fishing: nothing only a few perch. Her father was on his knees, trying to shut a big old suitcase but the rusty hasps would not fasten. He took a knife and they went out to the cart house for a bit of an old harness strap. Quick! It was my idea suddenly—Why? With my penknife I gutted the perch, parcelled the guts in a sheet of an old *Western People*, wrote TO HANNAH A SECRET GIFT WITH ALL MY LOVE and shoved it well down into her case.

Click! We were back in Dublin when her letter arrived. '. . . And didn't I open the case at Crewe and see the lads' present. Well laugh. And me thinking it was something great. Well if I had them. It gave me a good laugh anyway and I landed at the convent safe and sound T. God . . . .'

'What present?' My mother smiled, until I told her.

The first thing I had noticed when I came back from Mayo was that we had got television. I had walked into the sitting room and seen the small black-and-white snowstorm in the corner—and then for some reason had run crying like a savage out into the back garden. Maybe that was why I was alone in the breakfast room that evening. It had become a sort of second kitchen, deserted at night, the grate empty, cold except for the glow of the Sacred Heart lamp.

Click! as my father came in, shutting the door behind him. He had a green bamboo from the conservatory in his hand. I knew. Mama had squealed. He was going to beat me like a dog.

'Did you . . . .?'

130

'I . . . .'

Whiu-thuh!

'Now will you . . . .' Whiu-thuh! Whiu-thuh!

'No! No!'

'Will you? Will you?'

'No! Never!' I had never known such pain. Whiu-thuh! Whiu-thuh! Whiu-thuh! Around the table, across the hearth, head banging against the Sacred Heart lampstand.

'You kneed me!'

'I did *not*. Now, will you . . . .?'

'Oh never.'

'Ever?'

'Never . . . never . . . .'

Palo of Billy Cotton's 'Waikey Wai-key!' carried in from the television in the sitting room as he went out, leaving me panting on the new rose petal-patterned carpet.

******

One evening I was in the study when I saw Paul come in the gate, stumbling with a large cardboard box. I let him in. The box was full of books, all the ones he had shown us that day in the flat. 'You'd never know . . . .' he tossed them onto the desk, '. . . you might find something in them.' There was a sheen of perspiration on his knotted forehead lines. 'Made a nice job of that—' He glanced about. 'I'll take the box.' Always that slight slight whine in his voice. 'Is Mama home?'

As she talked with him by the open hall door, I thought I heard him say but—a cross door banged shut—could not be sure: 'I am sorry.' He walked abruptly out to his bike.

I was putting the books up on shelves, looking at them—for suddenly, naturally, like a lock clicking to the last key in the ring, I knew he meant them for me; more, knew it was what I wanted—when I found a piece of paper marking a page in Eliot's *Four Quartets*, a sheet torn from an old exercise book, covered with Chinese characters. When I showed it to my mother, she told me what I should have guessed all along—that Paul had wanted to be a priest. A missionary, she said, but he had left the seminary because of the headaches he got there. He had turned to writing then, and had published stories, poems too; he had hung around with artists and all that type, she said. She had read one of his poems in *The Capuchin Annual*, but she remembered the title only, an Irish one, *An Spéir*. Then he had given it up and gone to London to *The Universe*.

She sent me over to his flat shortly afterwards with a tin of fairy cakes as a present but I got no reply. Another tenant coming out of the hall door, seeing me looking in the barred window, told me that Paul had left, leaving no forwarding address.

Good Counsel began arriving at our house again.

III

MARY COLE

13

Rattle the stick along the railings . . . . 1960 now.
　'Guess who's back?'
　'Who?'
　Gorman said 'O Braonain.'
　'Get lost.'
He was though, but when I went into class I hardly knew
him, except for the smile: so pale, his freckles had disappeared;
red-rimmed eyes with green-yellow like old sleep stuck in the
lashes. Everyone was crowding around him. He looked almost
dazed as he shook hands. The cuffs of a new green-and-check
sportscoat he wore almost hid his hands. When he spoke, I could
hardly hear him; sitting down, he put a hand to his temple as if
shading his eyes and did not speak again all day. He walked
home on his own. Gradually the priests stopped asking him
questions; soon we left him alone too. When he left again at the
end of term, I hardly noticed. I said, 'Where's O Braonain gone?'
to Gorman one day; he just shrugged.
　The Matric. was coming up. Every day the same grind—
grammar, unseens, texts over and over until we ran as smooth as
oil. Everyone passed, nearly everyone came back to sixth year.
Since first year we had been hearing about this from Father
Wilmot; when we finally got there, he had gone to America and,
in his place, in return, we had someone else—an American. ('Join
the Js, see the world,' O'Hara said.)
　Father Williams introduced him in one sentence, 'Father
MacNamara will be taking you for English', looked at us slowly
as usual, then left. We looked at Father MacNamara; he looked
at us. He had been ordained, so he must have been in his thirties,
but he seemed almost as young as we were. His forehead was

lightly lined but only, it seemed, from a habit of holding his eyebrows slightly raised. He sat at the rostrum table and crossed his legs. Under the table I could see his toe swing, almost as restlessly as my father's. Yet differently. There were different kinds of Jesuit, but the same calm. What was it? I had often wondered . . . . The day Father Rowan came into class with a black eye and, seeing our glances, had said 'I'd like you to remember at Rosary this morning a young man who is appearing in court'—he looked calmly at his watch—'about now.' It was ca-lm.

Father MacNamara glanced at his fingernails as if thinking of something to say. He asked us what we were going to do in university. We took in the light, indefinable accent.

Spring said 'Classics and law.' Sandys said 'Law.' MacGowan said 'Law'. Gorman said 'History'. O'Hara said 'Architecture'. I said 'History'. Johnson said 'Law'. MacDermot said 'Law'. Fitzgerald said 'Law'. O'Reilly said, 'The Bar, actually.'

Father MacNamara glanced at his fingernails again, then at a book he had on the table, a spotless, just-bought hardback, and said, 'I—em— thought you might be interested in this.' He ran his nails through his hair as he began to read to us. It was a novel called *Franny and Zooey*. He read all through class, and the next day and the next.

We were on the top floor now, looking out each day at rising clouds of sweet blue smoke. Father O'Conor had gone, the new rector was cutting down the jungle of old laurels that had walled the grounds. Fresh bonfires every day. You could see Shamrock Rovers' terraces now. For ten years we had been moving up slowly room by room through this old house. Everyone had said sometime or other what he was going to do, but it was only now, hearing all together the answers to Father MacNamara's question, that I took it in. Gorman had not changed, of course. O'Hara had been talking of Architecture—though he was draw-

135

ing still, painting too—but had not actually said it until now. And all the others: Spring, nibbling skin from about his fingernails . . . Sandys, gazing at his perfect hands . . . had they just said 'Law' as I had said 'History' because they did not know what to say?

'"Now don't you know who the Fat Lady really is?"' Father MacNamara's husky voice went on. He was absorbed by the book by now, did not even look up to see if we were interested. '"Ah, Buddy. Ah, Buddy. It's Christ Himself. Christ Himself, Buddy . . . ."'

'Quite obviously' MacGowan said, 'he's a brilliant man.'

'Because he can read?' O'Hara said.

MacGowan laughed, but O'Hara continued to look at him for an answer until MacGowan stuck his thumbs in his canary waistcoat pockets and drifted off to talk with Sandys.

'What did you think?' O'Hara turned to me, which was nice.

'*Catcher in the Rye* was better.'

'I haven't read it.'

It was nice because, by now, our class had divided and O'Hara was definitely on the right side, and I was not, although I was not as bad as Gorman who, as someone said, was 'as far out as Uranus'.

'It's in the RDS ,' Gorman appeared by my side. He spent most afternoons in the RDS library because, I suppose, he was never invited anywhere, not even to Saturday coffee in Switzers, never mind to parties. As he talked, flushing with excitement to O'Hara, I wondered how the sword fell like that—gradually or suddenly? leaving him on one side, O'Hara on the other. It did not seem a very hard question: falling gradually, in fact as long as I had known him seemed the obvious answer. But why had the sword landed so suddenly now, making the past ten years seem as unreal as the smoke drifting up past the windows?

My father in the conservatory, the glass door tight shut.

'Can I have the Mini tonight? I'm going to a party.'

'Who's going?' He put a hand in his pocket.

'Everyone, more or less.'

'Who're you going with?' He handed me the key ring. 'Anthony?'

'He's not going.' I must have smiled.

'Never drop old friends like that.' He snapped the newspaper up before his face—*The Irish Times* now, but the same old frieze of tots along the margin.

My father in the conservatory, my Aunt Josie's visits: that's what I think of when I think of Mary Cole.

' . . . The flail, that's what he had yet, the big old flail! As true as I'm sitting here, and the old dash-churn. Sure, he didn't know what a tin-opener was. Well, he's in Heaven now, may God have mercy on him . . . .' My Aunt Josie stopped for breath and I slipped into a chair beside my cousin, Sean, who was in mine, the one with the cushion.

'And how many times did I say to him "Lord God Almighty, can't you take the ESB, aren't you well able to afford it and not be sitting within in the dark?" And do you know what it is he used to say . . . .?'

'What?' My mother smothered a yawn, eyes still shining with curiosity for news of Home.

I had not been there since that afternoon we had visited, years ago, on our way to Connemara. But it had been there, I vaguely knew, from the presents that came: black blood puddings, or a pullet with its cloven head unplucked, a damp ball of turfmould caught in each claw, in parcels lined with the *Connaught Tribune*, ventilated by knife-stabs. More and more now they came by hand, and a strong hand it looked too, my Aunt Josie's. All the work it had done—sowing, killing, milking, plucking—

since I had seen it last. When my mother had gone home for her own mother's funeral, it had clenched into a fist that stopped her from going upstairs. 'For fear I'd steal something . . . .', my mother had cried when she told it, '. . . steal *from my own home* . . .' and yet, a few months later, she was writing Home again. Now that Home was here beside her, she looked as if she wished she could be on another planet, Uranus, if possible. What was it, I wondered—as I wondered about Jesuit ca-lm, about Law, about that dividing line—that tied her to Home?

'Would you like some pepper, Sean?' she reached across the table for something to do.

'Is it pepper in the egg?' Sean looked up slowly.

'He'll be next with the notions.'

'Just turn the roundy part at the top, love.' My mother turned to me. 'Sean's going into the army, isn't that nice?'

'The cadet college,' my Aunt Josie laughed, 'if you don't mind.'

'What's that?'

'That's for the officers!' Aunt Josie laughed again, showing her even teeth. 'The officers.'

My cousin Sean ate steadily, his gaze moving about the room, resting on each little thing—the cedar candlestick . . . the glass lamp. They might not have been there, all my father's antique shop booty, they were so familiar now. Now Sean's steady gaze lit them up one by one like a torch beam and passed on.

'What're you going on for yourself?' The beam turned on to me.

'History.' I tried to turn the beam back on him. 'What part of the army will you be in?'

'Cavalry.' He turned the mill with powerful hands, smiling down at the little shower of black pepper. I quailed.

'Why don't you go for a walk with Sean?' my mother said.

138

'And ye can have a right old chat!'

'I have to go out.'

'Where?'

'Isn't he all right!' My Aunt Josie laughed. 'Won't we be up again!'

'Browne's having a supper party.'

'Indeed!' My Aunt Josie laughed once more. 'Haven't we come a long way from home!'

'That's what I meant to ask you—' My mother took the needle she kept under the tablecloth for picking her teeth, held its shining point to the light. '—How did Katie Fahy die?'

The dividing line was as absolute as a frontier, and as mysteriously irregular, until you knew the rules. Looks and money helped, old money helped even more, and style. But one without the others was not enough. When Browne was handing out invitations to his party, he had smiled at Gorman and the unlucky few—a helpless kind of smile like a Customs man presented with an irregular passport. But, like a frontier, there were other crossing points. Browne and I were friends because we went shooting together. Ever since that first Diana, I had had some sort of gun, a .410 at the moment. Together in the dark in Booterstown marsh, we blazed at wild duck coming in off the sea.

The house was lit up, the party well started, when O'Hara and I arrived. Down in the basement, their pointer was baying as the noise grew overhead. Browne was bounding about in great form. In class Father MacNamara had given up before he got to Browne; if he had asked, he would have got the most amazing answer of all—Photography. Alone of all our class, Browne was not going to university. His father, who lectured there, was arranging for him to go to South America for a year to think things over. Meanwhile, Browne was getting his own back in advance. A girl he had met in a camera shop had turned up. Introducing her to his father brought a healthy flush to his sallow cheeks.

'Daddy—Judy.'

'That's me.' She had a full husky Dublin accent. She was a beauty with cream hair and cheeks, and a brown knitted dress that clung to her thighs.

'Good, good.' Mr Brown smiled a distant, Brazilian smile.

Father MacNamara was there too, uneasy in his party posture: one leg stiff straight, the other limp alongside; one hand straight down in his jacket pocket, the other leaning a gin and tonic against his black lapel. And MacGowan . . . O'Reilly . . . Sandys touching his hair back from his temple as he strolled gravely from group to group . . . all the cravats, as O'Hara called them. O'Hara could call them what he liked, they only liked him all the more.

'I liked that Salinger, father.' He crossed the room, a long one bright with silver, scented with the steaming wine cup a maid was ladling into glasses.

'I've em just got his latest.'

'Which one is that?'

"*Raise High the Roofbeam, Carpenters*"—Father MacNamara took out a packet of cigarettes and juggled with them and his gin and tonic as he tried to strike a match, "*—and Seymour; An Introduction*"

'Father!' Mrs Browne appeared, a tall handsome enameled-looking woman and led him across the hall. 'You know Sir Gilbert . . . .'

Looking out of the window, enjoying that nice stilt-high feeling a house over a basement gave, I could see across Dublin Bay a long lighted train strung out against the dark on its way to Howth Head where a full moon was rising. It made me think of

140

Gorman. Where was he this evening? Out walking with his father? I often saw them together, gloved hands swinging, talking as if they had only just met.

'Look here, everyone!' Mr Browne was folding back double doors into a back room where varnished floorboards sparkled with French chalk—'I want to start the dancing.' Through another open door, I saw a line of girls come down the stairs, amongst them Mary Cole, fair hair brushed shining. I tingled down to my feet. Though it felt like always, I had met her only twice: once at her school bazaar—she went to Leeson Street, where my sister went too—and once at a hockey match where I had actually spoken to her ('You're Sacred Heart, aren't you?').

'Ssssh!' Mr Browne was rattling a box of pennies, giving one to each couple he drew aside.

'Caroline, you know James . . . .'

'Caroline—Justin.'

So many girls were called Caroline.

'Mary—Adrian.' He placed a penny on my forehead and held it there as he pressed her forehead to mine. 'Ssssh! Sssh! Now, the last couple on the floor, the last couple that is to say—' Mr Browne lectured in Law '—with the penny still between their foreheads will have their photograph taken with this new "Polaroid" camera!' He lowered the record player needle.

'I suppose that's Hugh's camera,' Mary Cole breathed. 'Did you hear that he wants to be a *photographer?*'

'I think he wants to be a real photographer, Mary.'

'What's that, Adrian?' She stepped back, pressed close again as our penny slipped, and now she was so close I could feel her against me. Under her stiff dress, her body moved like sea water. 'Like an artist?'

'Something like that.'

Some couple's penny slipped, fell, then another. 'But—' she breathed seriously, 'is a photograph art?'

'Is it? I don't know, Mary.'

'I don't think so, Adrian.' Her perfume was faint but distinct as the tissue wrapping on an orange.

'But why?'

'Because it's just, well, it's just a *reflection*.'

'And what's art then, Mary?' It was amazing. A minute before I knew only her name and now we were wrapped about each other talking about art. 'I mean, what's the difference?'

'Art's beautiful, isn't it? That's what we were told at school.' Our penny was slipping again; we pressed closer. 'But a photo could be of . . . *anything.*'

The noise of pennies dropping everywhere now, like backing music to Acker Bilk's clarinet.

'Do you like this one?'

'I only like "Stranger on the Shore".'

We were pressed so close together that when the music stopped and our names were called out and we stood apart, there was a circle mark on her forehead. I must have had the same. Mr Browne put the penny in his pocket and took our photo with the new camera. By the time it came slithering out, the proper dancing had begun. Mary Cole and I went back to the drawing room and sat on a couch to look at the glistening black-and-white print.

'Would you like to have it?'

'Are you sure?' she said.

'Do. I don't want it.'

'Thank you very much,' she said coolly.

'I mean, I want you to have it!' Hellish silence then for a minute. Through the folded back doors, I watched Browne doing a one hand jive with Judy.

'All right.' She had a habit of stressing words. She smiled and drew back an invisible strand of hair from her forehead. That was another habit she had.

'Cole, T.C.P, B.L., 4 Pembroke Villas, Ball's Bridge 67542.'

'67542—' I shut the directory, '67542—' and listened at the breakfast room door.

'—But do you know the ones that really make me laugh?' my Aunt Josie was up again, making plenty of noise, thank God. 'The connoiseurs! I do be looking at them there in The Imperial sipping the glass of wine—' smick-smack of lips '—and, of course, they no more know . . . .'

'67542 . . . .' I tiptoed back to the telephone.

'Hello?'

'Is that the Cole residence?'

'I beg your pardon?'

'Is Mary there?'

'Will I say who?'

'Could you say Adrian?'

'Adrian, could you hold the line?'

'Good man yourself,' Mr Heathley said down from his ladder. The painters were in too, making plenty of noise, thank God.

'Hello?' The serious voice was chilling.

'Hello! I was wondering if we could meet in town? For coffee? Remember we met at Browne's party? This is me. Adrian.'

'Hello, Adrian.'

'Can you?'

'Oh, I don't know.'

'Oh do.'

'When?'

'Saturday?'

'*Saturday!* Where?'

'Say, Switzers?'

'*Switzers!* When?'

'After school? Say, three?'

'Well, I'll *see.*'

'You're laughing,' Mr Heathley said. He turned back to his work, dipping the brush carefully into gold paint, drawing it over a lamp bracket.

'How did you find my number?'

'You told me. I looked under "T".'

She smiled, opened her coat and settled it about her. She was still wearing her uniform, the winter one—all navy but for a single crimson braid. 'I ought to be studying really.'

'Would you like to order something?'

She shook her head. I said, 'What will you do after your Leaving?'

'I told you. French and Italian.'

'For the summer, I mean.'

'I'm going to Italy.'

'For what?'

'To learn Italian. I went last year.'

'Did you like it?'

'Everyone likes Italy.'

'What was it like?'

'I was with a family.'

'What were they like?'

'Such questions! It wasn't really a family—just a husband and wife. And he kept *following* me about the house. I'd *die* if I were married to someone like that.'

'Are you sure you wouldn't like something?'

'*Let's.*' She looked about her. 'I was never here before. Look, the waitress's uniform is practically the same as ours!'

144

'Yours.'

Her cheeks blushed as red as the braid.

'I think you're very nice.'

She drew back an invisible strand of hair from her forehead. 'I'll send you a card from Italy, will I?'

'But I'll see you before that?'

'Ssh,' she said as the waitress appeared.

I did not see her again until after her Leaving, and then only for a minute in, of all places, Rathmines Castle. It had been sold and its land—flats were *the* danger now, Mr Corcoran said—and everything in it was being sold. Everyone was at the auction. She was with her mother, I was with mine. I had time only to hear that she had passed and was off to Italy, then the crowd carried her past. When I waved, the auctioneer looked at me, my mother panicked and bid for two chairs that were being held up. They were dining-chairs but their backs, as straight and solid as their seats, cut into our backs and they ended up in the hall, one either side of the telephone table.

'Hello?'

Sometimes, when the phone rang and it was a trunk call, I had the mad idea it might be her, in spite of her 'I never telephone boys', calling me from Italy. Then the slow crashing in of coins from the other end. It was not until I got her card—she had drawn it herself, 'Three Clumsy Graces' in the same slatey ink they used at school, saying she would be back before it—that I stopped expecting to hear her voice.

'Hello! Who's that?'

'Is that you, Aunt Josie?'

'Well, you're as clear! You'd think you were here beside me!'

'I'll be in the conservatory,' my father said.

The conservatory had become his, though there was nothing to show it, unless the bareness. No flowers, just light and the shadows of the roof-joists like ribs across the wall. What was he thinking of sitting there with his fingers joined?

'Have you a moment?'

Not even a musky geranium; just the austere warm-body smell.

'Have you been looking ahead at all?'

'Not really. I thought I'd go to university.'

'With a view to—?' He interrupted himself. 'I've complete confidence in you—' His shoe began to swing. He was wearing his red socks. '—But I don't want you to be going too deep. That was half Paul's trouble, you know. He went too deep.'

I tried to change the subject. 'How is he?' For Uncle Paul had had another accident.

'Ah, all right. He'll be all right.'

His motor bike, a new Honda 50, had gone on fire—' burst into flames,' it had said in a small newspaper report, outside *The Irish Times* office in D'Olier Street.

'I don't want you to come into the business, you know.'

'Yes.'

'Unless you want to.'

'No.'

'That's all right, that's all right. What I'd like you to do is '— he opened his hand and looking at them, long heavy fingers, scored thumbnail across the face of thumb— 'something . . . .'

'History, I was thinking of.'

'Fair enough.' He joined his hands again.

I shut the glass door and slipped away to read another of Uncle Paul's deep books, *The Gum Trees* by Roy Campbell, Drawings by David Jones.

14

'It's just off Harcourt Street.' He caught my sportscoat by the collar, tugged my new camel hair overcoat straight at the back. *'Harcourt Street.'*

I knew the city backwards about his shoe shops, and the bookshop quays where you had to lock your bike. Off Harcourt Street my world ended. I cycled off the edge of the map down silent wide redbrick streets, each vista closed by an unfamiliar shape: a handsome shut church, a gasometer. I was lost, I realised, as I cycled around St. Stephen's Green. Cycling around the second time I saw a Guard outside Foreign Affairs who walked with me to the corner of Earlsfort Terrace. A college porter showed me up some back stairs to a theatre and I sat into the last bench.

Far below were rows of clerical students; behind them nuns, then girls—there was Mary Cole's fair hair tied up in a big loose knot; and behind them boys—there was Gorman's head. The lecturer was scanning a line from Ovid's *Metamorphoses* on the blackboard. I turned to the boy sitting beside me. He was older-looking, with a black beard, and on the ledge in front of him instead of a notebook was a small green felt hat with feathers in the band. We began to chat—his name was Roderick, he was English, his father was Irish—until the lecturer looked up at us. Roderick took a notebook from under the hat, put the hat on his head.

'Take off that hat, please!' the lecturer called up.

'Sorry!' Roderick said. I felt straightaway we were going to be friends when he put the hat back on the notebook.

We went downstairs together afterwards. Flagged in black-

and-white, the main hall floor was like a full chessboard. Sandys and MacGowan, in green and purple law scarves already, were moving from square to square. Gorman came over with someone he had met.

'This is Roger. I'm sorry— didn't get the first name.'

Roger looked even younger than I did, with long baby blonde hair. He said 'Murphy' in an English public school drawl.

'Where're you from?' Roderick asked. He had a slightly different accent.

'Yorkshire. What about you? Nottingham? Stafford?'

'Chee-hee-hee!' Roderick laughed like they laughed in *The Beano* and said, 'Not bad! Not bad! Derbyshire actually.'

'Is the hat from Derbyshire too?'

'Don't you like it?' Roderick patted it down. 'I got it in Austria.'

'It's ghastly. What are you doing here?'

'I couldn't get into Trinity.'

'Same here. Where were you at school?'

'Stonyhurst. What about you?'

'Ampleforth,' Roger said.

This was amazing. Amazingly attractive too. Sandys and MacGowan joined our square, talking with Roger—he was doing Law, he said. They frowned awkwardly as he pressed palms together making realistic farting noises, and moved on to another square.

'Where're you staying?' Roderick asked.

Roger said 'Synge Street. It's vile.'

'I'm looking for a place. If you fancy sharing, we could get something OK together.'

'OK.'

This was incredible. Then O'Hara appeared, a striped Architecture scarf twisted twice around his long neck, a T square like a signpost over his shoulder. He lit himself a Carrolls and, when

Roger asked to try one, he passed the packet around—and now I was smoking too, almost floating like the smoke, when I saw Mary Cole come over to join us. She was dressed, like all the other girls I had noticed, as if for a wedding, in high heels, nylon stockings, best costume and handbag. When Roderick said, 'What about a spot of drink?', she said, 'What about the Mass?'

'What's this?' Roderick looked at her through his thick glasses. Between them, the hat and beard, it was hard to see much of him.

'There's a notice in the ladies' sitting-room. It's for the start of term.'

We noticed then other groups moving across the chessboard floor and followed them down a stairs and out a door, across a yard and in a gate to a gardens where I could see what a large crowd there was ahead; flowing past cement classical statues, in another gate, down steps and into a basement filled with cabbage steam, up to a classical hall, out another door and I saw we were in St. Stephen's Green where I had got lost that morning. By then the church was full, leaving a small crowd swirling about outside, as if there was indeed a wedding. Mary Cole stood by the door, shoes close together.

'Not bad,' Roderick said aside.

'*Bad*.' Roger echoed the flat vowel.

It was all as new to us as to them. Together we looked at the lead lion on the portico, the three bronze Fates in the Green, the Boer War arch—which Roderick pointed through with his umbrella. 'This way! I was down here yesterday. Bought this brolly as a matter of fact.'

Every day he tried carrying it in a new way, swinging it along before him, then holding it like a newspaper under his arm, then like a spear upright, then like a rifle on his shoulder. By Christmas it had disappeared.

Halfway down Grafton Street, he put his head into a bookshop, where a girl smiled and said, 'It hasn't come in yet.'

'Vasari's *Lives*, Roderick explained.

'Of the artists?' O'Hara saved us from disgrace.

'That's it! Very good, sport! You've got to know your stuff!' Roderick led the way into the Bailey. 'Yes, you need the old classical tradition behind you.' He leaned back against the bar. 'I mean—'

I wished he would keep his voice down . . . just a little. A man with a face of indescribable bitterness, holding a pint steady, winked at me as Roderick mused at the top of his voice.

'—Take Brunelleschi . . . . Are you familiar with the Dome in Florence?'

'No,' I muttered. If only to God that man would go away. Mary Cole ordered a Tio Pepe but her voice was drowned by Roderick's.

'—Vasari says they wanted him to show his model for the Dome, but Brunelleschi wouldn't. He said whoever could stand an egg on a flat piece of marble should get the commission. So they got an egg and all the other architects tried to stand it on end and couldn't. Then Brunelleschi took the egg—'

The man paused with the pint to his lips and leaned closer, listening intently. I gazed away in a frenzy of tension as Roderick's voice filled the bar. '—And just cracked the bottom of it on the marble and stood it upright! Chee-hee-hee!'

Mary Cole said, 'But that was *cheating.*'

'That's what the others said! They said anyone could do that and Brunelleschi said, 'You'd have said the same thing if I showed you my model.'

'Why buy Vasari,' Roger drawled once more, 'if you know it so well?'

'My books are in England.' Like a swallow gliding round a gable, Roderick turned to the bar. 'Wine? Any wine?'

By the time we got back to college, I was late for lectures

again.

The weeks flew by, marked by Roderick's umbrella, forever moving like a large clock hand. Every day there was something new to talk about. Roderick saw everything through those thick glasses. When a girl came into the library one morning wearing blue jeans, a red-spotted handkerchief tied about her neck, he was the one to notice, nudging me just in time before the librarian saw her and sent her home. He had an opinion on everything too; the same opinion in different shapes. I noticed gradually.

'Of course, Catholicism is just a sheen on the Classical Tradition—' Roderick's lecture began almost before our lecturer had left the room. '—like the beautiful green scum on an old church dome. Take the Pantheon . . . .'

'Take a peasant—' Half Bewley's café turned to the loud voice. '—send him a letter, what does he do? Read it and throw it in the fire? No. He puts it back in the envelope, stands it on the mantelpiece like a picture. He's literally illiterate. All great literature had that great dark substratum, that . . . .'

Gradually O'Hara's cool gaze turned into an open smile, Gorman began to argue back, Roger yawned. I didn't care. I liked Roderick only as a fellow-sufferer could, although it was Mary Cole who diagnosed the complaint one foggy evening as we walked around the Green through the dead leaves and his name came up yet again. She sniffed and said, 'A jackdaw with peacock's feathers.'

15

'Adrian!'

No, I'm not going to Mass this morning . . . . It sounded so easy, I said it aloud to my reflection in the mirror, using my reflection as my mother. 'No, I'm not going to Mass this morning.'

What would she say? I wondered as I washed my teeth. Cry? Faint?—I slumped to the floor, but even as I watched my reflection slump. I knew that that too was far below the mark.

Tear out her hair? Scream?—Not enough, not enough, I knew. With the toothbrush for a knife, I watched my reflection drive stabs through the heart, stomach, breast. That was getting closer, I felt as I watched the coup de grâce—a slow slash across the throat.

'Adrian!'
'What?'
'It's twenty past!'
'Coming!'

Gorman and O'Hara went to Rathgar church too. After Mass, before the feast of rashers and sausages, we hung around the cement-renaissance façade talking about college. School had dropped right out of sight, though when I mentioned that Father MacNamara had left and gone back to America, O'Hara began one of his MacGowan imitations.

'Quite obviously he's a brilliant man.'

'And Browne went to South America,' Gorman interrupted.

'To think things over,' O'Hara smiled cigarette smoke down

his nostrils. 'It's like the Middle Ages.'   And now he was imitating Father Rowan in History class. 'Your father was a stone mason, *you* became a stone mason . . . .'

'Where does that leave you?'

'Can you see me as a judge?'

'Your father's the only one I've seen.'

O'Hara took another drag on his fag. He did not talk much about architecture. At night when I passed his house, he was always up in his room—lit by a lamp so bright I could see the lines on his drawing-board, but between lectures he always drifted over to us in the main hall. 'I hear Roderick and Roger found a flat. I wouldn't say No to that.'

'Where?'

'Appian Way.' I passed on the rumour of a party.

'That's more like it,' Gorman said. He'd a lot more to say lately, even read a paper to the History Society. He went over to the railings to buy *The Sunday Times*. So did O'Hara, so did I and we walked back Frankfort Avenue together, reading Cyril Connolly's article on Louis MacNeice, who had died.

'He made a right mess of his life, I believe, poor chap.' O'Hara looked up as we passed Uncle Paul's old flat, imitating again—a suddenly irritating habit.

Saturday, after dinner—we had dinner in the evening now— Gorman called for me and together we called for O'Hara. As usual he got up when we came in, eager to get out, and then, as Mrs O'Hara offered us sherry, as Mr O'Hara said '*Jim*' , he slid down insolently slowly into his chair again, scratching the back of his head along Lecky's *History*.

'Who's giving this party?'

'A couple of English fellows,' O'Hara said. 'It makes a

153

change.'

'From what?'

'They're different.'

'In my experience,' Mrs O'Hara said, 'the English have about as much individuality as locusts.'

'Yes, they're English first . . . .' Mr O'Hara began.

'And human beings second.' Mrs O'Hara concluded.

'These are half-Irish.' O'Hara gazed at the ceiling. I could never understand why he was so bored here where things were talked about so briskly.

In the hall, as he tied himself up in his duffle coat—with the hood he looked like a monk—he raised his eyes to heaven, but got no sympathy from us. Sherry! Compared with our *Quosh*, diluted by Dr Gorman as if it was whiskey, O'Hara was in clover.

One thing we had in common was Art, whose name had been in the papers. He had just been jailed for burglary. We had not seen him since he had left school and yet we talked about him all the way down Palmerston Road.

'I suppose he could say he's done Law,' said O'Hara. Yet he too was impressed, asking Gorman, who had read the *Independent* report, for more details: the waiting squad car . . . the Justice's remarks—'I don't care *who* he is . . . .' It was strange to think that Art was sitting in a cell in Mountjoy while we walked to a party this windy night, yet not surprising. A real surprise, I decided, was not really 'surprising' at all; more something expected appearing suddenly, like the Winking Willie at the end of Palmerston road, lighting up everything in a strange new way.

Maybe that was why I was not all that surprised to see my cousin, Sean, at the party, though you don't have to be surprised to get a fright. Besides, Roderick and Roger had been inviting to it all week: people they had met at other parties—in Trinity, in someone's digs in Drumcondra, at a hunt ball in Kildare.

154

Sean did not seem all that surprised to see me either—just a hand upraised from the other end of the room, a ramshackle one with draughts skimming in under big windows and doors (the house would be levelled before we left college), gathering up the fire into a hoarse blaze. On the walls were previous tenants' leftovers: a poster photo of Pele scoring a goal, another of Michelangelo's *David*. This was different.

'Red or White?' Roderick was going around, a bottle of wine in each hand. A girl without shoes was lying on her side on a bed, Roderick's judging by the hat beneath it, and the books— *Southern Baroque, Some Do Not*. Roger was talking with Mary Cole and a boy in motor bike boots who, as we joined them, went over to talk to the girl on the bed. When she turned with a smile, I recognised her—it was Judy, the camera shop girl who had been at Browne's party. The boy in boots sat down beside her.

'He's at Trinity,' Roger said.

'Is it true that you can read *Private Eye* there?'

'I don't see what's so special about Trinity.' Mary Cole's face was red after a glass of wine. 'My father was at UCD. And my grandfather.'

'And?' O'Hara said.

'Well, I think it's all right, that's all.'

The Trinity boy in boots seemed to be doing all right, already stroking Judy's feet. I looked away as my cousin, Sean, appeared suddenly before me.

'How did you get here?'

' Roderick asked me.'

'Who's he?'

'That's me, sport.'

'I thought you were giving the party?' Sean turned to Roger, who straightened that one out, then yawned and said, 'Where's this we met?'

'Are you at Trinity too?' Mary Cole asked quite sharply.

'No no no.' Sean laughed, putting out a large hand, catching me firmly by the shoulder. 'Did he tell you we're cousins?'

That did not seem to interest O'Hara, who just said, 'What do you do?'

While Sean talked about horses and remembered where he had met Roger—the hunt ball—I got another look at Judy. The boy's hands were moving up her legs, caressing her thighs now, neither of them even glancing at Roderick as he reached under his bed for his hat. His hair was thinning on top, and I wondered again just how old he was.

'I don't know how a girl could let herself be treated like that,' Mary Cole murmured to me.

'No . . . no,' Judy sighed.

'His old man's a baronet,' Roderick said out of the corner of his mouth.

O'Hara's questions about the Curragh—'What do you do down there?'—slightly stressing the second 'do', rocking slightly from toes to heels as if he was on the end of a diving-board, were irritating Sean I could tell. His hand, still heavy on my shoulder, flexed, unflexed, as O'Hara went on in the same polite, fascinated way he used to ask questions of the gardeners at school. ('Which is the shovel—the *pointy* one?')

'And what do *you* do?' Sean turned slowly to face him.

'Architecture.' O'Hara scratched some part of his back between his shoulder blades, deliberately, as if illustrating the sort of work he did. This composure, everything about him in fact, seemed to irritate Sean more and more. It reminded me of the annual almighty quarrel my brother and I used to have with Margaret, which built up from anything and everything. Although the next ingredient was not all that everyday. A flushed middle-aged man came in.

'Joseph!'

Roderick raised his hat. 'My old landlord! How's the old man?'

'Still sitting in that chair.' Joseph had a New York accent. 'Still smoking those cigarettes.'

'Your father?' Gorman looked up.

'We came over together—got a flat in Joseph's house in—' Roderick tried it in Irish, gave up and said 'Dunleary.'

'Maybe you should've stayed.' Joseph looked about, then opened his raincoat—once white—and took out a small painting. 'I brought you a present.'

'Joseph's an artist,' Roderick said, casually as he passed around the canvas—unframed, showing close up, without background, a thatched whitewashed cottage.

'May I?' O'Hara took it, studying the paint, laid on it seemed with a knife. 'No door?' he smiled.

'Yes, where's the *door?*' Mary Cole said.

'It's the back of a house,' Joseph explained.

'That's very amusing!' She turned the canvas to show the blank back. 'And this is the *front!*'

'Where's the drink?' Joseph enquired.

'These cottages—do they really have no back door?' O'Hara turned to Sean again.

A huge silence then, or so it seemed to me. The fire roared. I tried to look interested in the fireplace, marble with a carved medallion showing a sleeping cherub; some tenant with a biro had given him a life-sized cock. Sean's hand lifted from my shoulder—for a moment, I thought, to hit O'Hara, but only to wave to a horsey-looking group coming in the door on another blast of freezing air, who called him—more English accents— 'John'.

'You tell me,' he said shortly to O'Hara who looked blankly at him. The wind was howling outside now, driving static through Radio Luxembourg music, almost drowning the horsey

English voices. This other little storm, I realised, was passing unnoticed over O'Hara's head, bent forward again to study Joseph's canvas.

For him a house was just a house: there was only one kind. For Sean, I realised with a qualm—it was like catching an unexpected glimpse of myself in a mirror—there were two: cottage and castle. He looked at O'Hara as uncomprehendingly as O'Hara looked at him, then shrugged his powerful shoulders and made across the room to the horsey people. In a minute, he was deep in chat with a girl in a plunged-neck dress.

'I like it.' O'Hara held the canvas at arm's length.

'Do you paint "full time"?' Mary Cole was asking Joseph.

He ran a hand through greying hair. She went on. 'I'm doing French and Italian. James,' she put a hand on O'Hara's shoulder, 'is doing Architecture. That's why he noticed about the *door!* '

'This one's a chateau—' Roderick flourished a bottle upside down, filling glasses all around. His bed was creaking now as Judy and the boy in boots—trousers loosened, showing a flash of red underpants—rolled in embrace.

'I have to be up in the morning.' Mary Cole looked at her watch.

'What's first tomorrow?' Gorman scratched his head. 'Mediaeval Europe?'

'Mass,' O'Hara said.

'Monday, I mean.' After ten years of *Quosh*, the wine was too much for him. For me too. Faces were blurring, the flat was filling up, people were starting to dance. Someone was frying an egg in the kitchen. Loud scraps of conversation mixed with the drink roar in my ears.

'I see myself as European,' someone was saying in a Radio Eireann voice.

'I'm going,' Mary Cole announced.

A small strange thing as I went to the bathroom, where the

158

coats lay in a haycock heap: Sean was standing at the lavatory, holding himself I could not help noticing as you would hold a cigar. Unconcerned, he turned to me—'How's your mother?'

'OK. How's yours?'

'They don't hit it off, do they?'

'True.'

As if ash from the cigar, he tapped off a lingering drop and winked. And, with the sort of relief I felt when Austin arrived home and our ancient row with Margaret ended, I winked back.

The wind was at our backs as we linked down Appian Way , Mary and I; throwing wet leaves before us, undoing her hair from its big loose knot.

'Did you like that party?'

'Yes. Did you not?'

'Not really.' She added, 'I hate parties like that.'

'I was never at one like that.'

More silence. We turned into Morehampton Road. Then—'Your cousin's nice. It's nice to see someone Irish. All those West British—who do they think they are?'

'Joseph isn't.'

'I didn't think that picture was anything to write home about.'

'O'Hara did. He's Irish too.'

'You know what I mean.'

'And Gorman.'

'Maybe it needs a *frame*.' She stopped as we came to her house, hall door lantern shining through the lime tree branches clashing in the wind.

'What are you doing tomorrow?'

'I have to read *Les Enfants Terribles*.

'Have you seen *The Virgin Spring*?'

'I *beg* your pardon?'

'The Bergman film.'

'Oh, she's beautiful. I saw her in *The Inn of the Sixth happiness.*'

'That's Ingrid, Mary. This is Ingmar.'

'I beg your pardon.' She said it differently, blushing in the light streaming from her home.

'It's on in The Eblana if you'd like to come.'

She paused, turning down the collar of her coat, the same burnt cream colour as her hair. 'Let's!'

'I'll give you a ring.'

She gave me a shining misty smile and, as I leaned closer, put out her hand for me to shake Goodnight. She turned up the noisy gravel path to her door and I turned home, taking my time along all those roads I was getting to know—Pembroke . . . Clyde . . . Morehampton again, past Father Williams coming out of the Royal Hospital, head down over his bicycle lamp as he pushed against the gale . . . Marlborough . . . going over the evening in my mind—Sean, Judy, a baronet's son, an artist—a brilliant jigsaw . . . and still Father Williams was alongside, bicycle chain creaking taut. He did not see me; I did not like to speak. Side by side we went. Where was he coming from? A death bed? A recovery? Impossible to tell from his expression. It made me think of a time he gave out to us for the way we treated our books, telling us that the copy of Xenophon he had at school was the same copy his father had used; chatting to us then, telling how once as a boy he had lifted a barbed wire to let a Sinn Feiner on the run pass under and had been given a live bullet in thanks. Even then it had struck me that his voice was the very same telling the Xenophon story and the story of the live round. Or the other way round?

Black, spare as the bicycle, he pressed across Sandford Road and the red rear light vanished up the school avenue, a pinprick in the plunging spire-high tree shadows.

160

Or the other way round? That was a thought. I stuck my nose an inch out into gale. Or the other way round? And so I made my way home, in the newly painted sidegate and matching mushroom side door.

'Who were you with till this?' Getting ready for bed, getting ready for breakfast, my mother hovered in the kitchen, taking butter from the fridge so it would not be hard in the morning, and the milk, the eggs. 'Who?'

The name was what she wanted. The name. In the name of Jesus Christ, the name.

'Father Williams,' I said.

'You've a queer sense of humour.' She laid a muslin over all.

Queer . . . Qualm . . . Quarrel . . . Quosh . . . the words went round in my head as I went to sleep.

16

My father in the office, lips moving silently behind the glass. Mr Sinnot and a new girl were leaning against the shelves.

'The happy man. Always a smile on the jaw. How old are you now?'

The new girl said, 'I don't even know his name.'

'Adrian. Eighteen.'

'That's a great name.'

'What's yours'.

'Colette. Seventeen.'

My father put down the phone and they stood up straight. The shop looked busy, but was empty except for a woman, a walking-stick, a Yorkshire terrier and shopping bags. Mrs Morgan was kneeling before her. There were shoe boxes open all over the floor.

'How does that feel?'

'That's the eight?'

'That's the eight.'

'It feels a bit loose. Where's the seven?'

'That's the seven on your other foot.'

'And how much is that?'

'Nineteen and eleven. The same.'

'Could I see the six again?'

Colette leant back against the shelves again. 'Working here for Christmas, are you, Adrian?'

'Adrian *Kenny*' Mr Sinnot said and Colette looked at her shoes.

'CAN YOU NOT FIND SOMETHING TO DO?' my father murmured. He swung aside a hanging sheet of *Stubbs Gazette*. 'I THINK THE SIX MIGHT DO, MRS MORGAN.'

'It's just the tiniest bit . . . .'

'I'll put it on the stretching-machine,' Mrs Morgan said and I escaped with her down to the stockroom.

'Here.' She handed me a broom, stuck the toe of the shoe on top of the handle, tucked the shoe between her thighs. 'Push.'

I blushed as red as Colette and gazed away at the shelves of shoes I knew nothing about . . . Norvic . . . Winstanley . . . Lee . . . and thought of Mary Cole. *The Virgin Spring* . . . *Wild Strawberries* . . . *La Strada* . . . and still not even a kiss. From the moneylender's office behind the wall of shoes came sudden angry shouts, then the snarl of the alsatian, then Mr Reuben's quiet voice.

'Push.' Mrs Morgan squatted, her black skirt riding up her thighs. 'And how's Mrs Kenny? I never see her.'

'She was in town this morning. At Mass.'

'We might be lucky so.' She flipped the shoe in the air as she went back to the shop. 'Now . . . how does that feel?'

'That's the six?'

'That's the six. Walk up and down the shop till I see it on you.'

'You don't have it in anything plainer?'

'They all have the toe. That's all the go now.'

'I got a lovely little pair of slip-ons here once. They were as comfortable! I wore them to Mass and everywhere.'

Mrs Morgan went up the high ladder and came down with more boxes under her chin.

'Here's a very dressy little one.'

'A six?'

My father stepped out of the office, temple tic throbbing like the Horn of Moses.

'Have a look into Connolly's, would you?'

There was another shoe shop next door. I lounged outside like a customer. Full. I went back into ours. 'Empty,' I said.

163

Mr Sinnot was saying, 'That's the one for you.'

The woman said, 'The left one is a bit tight.'

'That'll wear off in a couple of days.'

'It's this little corn . . . . You couldn't sell me a six in the right and a seven in the . . . .'

Slam! My father left the shop, crossed the street and vanished up to Mr Cohen's antique shop. Mrs Morgan went up the ladder again, higher this time, higher until the veins bulging out of the backs of her legs were out of sight. This time she came down with a pair of pink slippers in her hand.

'What's this?' The woman slipped it on her bulging foot.

'A five.' Mrs Morgan walked on all fours alongside her, head down. 'And you've lots of room.'

'A *five* . . . .'

Mrs Morgan hummed softly, like Petie when he was trying to catch the piebald mare. Colette came slowly from behind with a mirror. Mr Sinnot bent and took the woman's old shoes. I patted the terrier's head.

'They're nice, mind you.'

'Will I wrap them up? Or would you rather . . . ?'

The woman's hand was opening her bag . . . taking out her purse . . . opening a safety pin . . . opening the purse . . .

'Isn't it unnatural weather?' Mrs Morgan was taking the money from her hand.

'Christmas. I hate it.' A ten shilling note . . . a two shilling piece . . . another . . . a threepenny bit. No wild hare sitting in Margaret's field was as beautiful as this silver one sitting in Mrs Morgan's hand.

'Sure, it's only for the children.'

'I'll have to leave you the penny short.'

'And a Merry Christmas to you.' Mrs Morgan was gently opening the door, shutting it quickly as the woman went out, away down the street, the slippers' pink poms winking out of

164

sight.

'She's from the country.' Mrs Morgan lay, weary, back again the shelves, blocking a yawn with her shoe-horn, the Dubliner explaining all.

The telephone rang in the office. Mr Sinnot nodded to me.

'Hello?'

'Dada?'

'It's me.'

'Your voice—it's got as deep . . . .' My mother lowered her voice. 'Remind him to get the marzipan. For the icing. For the cake.'

'OK.'

'Are you busy?'

'No.'

'Take care would you say that to him.'

'What?'

'Ooh!' She slammed down the phone.

'Lamb's heart—stuffed.' Mr Sinnot said it again, singing it almost as he put on his coat and went out. Mrs Morgan and Colette went down to the stockroom to make tea. I leant against the shelves—dazed as always by my mother's voice from no-where—watching the feet go by. Feet everywhere, striding, strolling, shuffling past the door, slipping in Reuben's back door, creaking on the floorboards overhead. Those were the times I thought of Mary Cole, longed to hear her clear voice.

'Hello?'

'Is Mary there please?'

'She is, Adrian. One minute please.'

If only our phone at home was in a glass box like this. I reclined on my father's high stool. In a way, his office was like

home. Pay Margaret . . . Pay Peter . . . Pay Paul . . . my hand
fidgeted through bundles of cashed cheques. Old family letters
too. I recognised Petie's National School writing on a sheet of
filthy paper hacked-jagged as if by a shears: '. . . Well the yeowes
are lambed and I have ease it was such a hard winter but I was
lucky enough I only lost two lambs I have seven lambs thank for
the coat . . . .'

'Hello!'

'Hello!'

'Where *are* you?'

'In town.'

'I'm just going *into* town!'

'Really!'

'Daddy's calling. I have to go now.'

The shop door opened. My father came in with Mr Sinnot.
'So have I.'

'Really!'

'The money's there,' Mr Sinnot said.

'There's a few bob stirring all right. Open the door,' my
father said. 'If it's only to let in the crows.'

A man walked in and bought a pair of shoes without even
trying them on.

'Thanks be to Christ for the single man.'

'There'll be another now,' Mrs Morgan said. 'wait till you
see.'

Then another, another, another—all at once the shop was
full. Then empty again, like a sea pool. But there was another
wave behind, bigger again and again. Feet, feet, feet. All year I
took them for granted, noticed faces, hands. Now it was foot
time. Long-toed, like chimpanzee's . . . dainty . . . dirty as if they'd
been uprooted from the earth.

'What that one wants is a blacksmith.' Mrs Morgan com-
mented on each as she shot the dockets into the office. We had

been busy at Christmas before, but this—

'There's a—' my father shook his head, uneasily almost '—change.'

You could feel it, like the muggy west wind turning into rain. Outside, the pavement between the traders' stalls and shop windows was packed. The street lights came on, shining the wet fruit and holly. My fingers were bleeding from trying to snap parcel twine.

'We'll have a great little country yet,' my father said, 'if they leave it to Lemass.'

'It's as good as the bloody War.' Mr Sinnot went out to the porch for a cigarette and a cough.

'You have to get the icing.'

He pressed money still warm from someone's pocket into my hand, and then— 'You can knock off now' - Lady Lavery's head in brown, a five pound note.

Muffled music of feet everywhere in the dark. Down the dark lane the money-lender's was packed. So was Connolly's next door; but so was our other shop down the street. So was the bakery at the back. Even Mr Groombach was smiling under his shapeless white hat. He gave me the marzipan, I pressed silver into his hand, warm foot money.

'How eez Missis Kenny?'

'Grand.'

'I nevair see her.'

Out into the dark again, down Camden Street, feet feet feet, into Montague Street. A messenger boy stood outside Mr Elkinson's money office, looking sad, a single pound note in his hand. Along the Green, down Grafton Street, the traffic jammed, up blaring horns at down, people pouring across from one shop into another; even into my father's brand new shop—I looked in and , instead of the usual sight, a woman alone holding a snakeskin shoe to the light, saw a score of them ankle deep in

167

empty boxes and tissue paper.

'*Hello!*'

Across the street, through the stand-still traffic, with her father came Mary Cole, a silk pink scarf half-covering her burnt cream hair that sparkled with rain.

'I was just talking about you to—what's this that English boy's name is?'

'Roderick?'

'The other one. He's going home for Christmas.'

'That's what's so pleasant about Dublin.' Mr Cole took his umbrella, the handle of jungle yellow bamboo, in his left hand. 'You meet everyone!' He held out his right to shake mine. 'Now which Kenny are you? Not Bill's?'

'No,'

'Paddy's? Paddy and I were called to the Bar together.'

'I don't think I'm any particular Kenny.' A voice, unbidden, from the foot world. Awful silence.

Mr Cole smiled shyly. 'I stand abashed.'

'Are you just *beginning* your shopping?' Mary Cole looked at my mother's molten marzipan with real concern.

'Well, I've got *my* present,' Mr Cole said.

'He insisted I buy him a Sir Walter Scott.'

'You must drop around after Christmas.' Mr Cole raised his umbrella again. 'Where,' he added shyly as another elbow caught him in the back, 'are all these people coming from?'

'A Happy Chrismas.' Shifting all her parcels, so many that, in such high heels, it seemed the wet wind might blow her over, she held out her hand for me to shake.

******

'Happy Christmas.'

My mother put a finger to her lips. 'Go into the sitting room.'

My father was standing by the fire, with a brand new shotgun. When he smiled, I knew the gun was for me. 'Watt said it was a good one.' He watched me as I took it up. 'What do you think?'

I ran a finger along a pointer, foot raised, rigid before game, engraved on the sidelock. 'It's heavy.'

He tapped the stock. 'That's walnut.'

I raised the gun to my cheek, sighting out the window while I thought of something to say. The thing was, I realised it only now, I was not interested in shooting any more. Tranquilla convent's bell rang.

'The cartridges are in the study.'

'I have to go to Mass.'

'You can always exchange it.' A touchy flush came to his forehead.

Damn damn . . . . I went up the road under the bare trees and tv aerials. Another strand of barbed wire topped Tranquilla's boundary wall. Ahead of me went O'Hara, dufflehooded. I had not seen much of him lately. He joined us less and less now in the main hall between lectures; yet did not hang around with the architects either. He was going to the convent chapel this morning. I followed him, through the wicket, set open in the big timber gate for this special hour, up the evergreen avenue and into the chapel—a small bare one with a lattice along one side of the chancel, through which the nuns could follow the Mass, through which we could see their shapes when they drew close to receive communion. Year by year I counted them—16 . . . 14 . . . 13 . . . fewer every year. But not this morning. Gosh—from a jutting-out rod like a flagpole hung a black sheet cutting off even that glimpse—not ever again.

'In nomine Patris . . . .' Father Cuthbert bowed before the altar and we knelt down, O'Hara resting his head in his hand.

Gosh—why was that?

169

17

Grandma, lying in a bed made up in the parlour, looking up at the ceiling, singing a verse of a hymn aloud; opened her eyes wider when I took her hand, white as the ceiling, to shake and began to ramble again. 'Good girl yourself! Who is she at all? hasn't she the lovely voice, God bless her!'

'Sit up and take something.' Grimly, Margaret lifted her up on the pillow and fed her a morsel of meat, and like the sun slipping through ink and pink evening clouds outside, her mind cleared for a moment, the hard little hand clutched mine. 'We always had chicken the sixth of January. And three cakes. Ever.'

'Why?'

' Blackcurrant . . . ginger . . . and caraway.'

'For what?'

'She's stone deaf,' Margaret said. 'For the Three Wise men. Why don't you have your hair cut?'

'It's not long.'

'It's silly. It's like a girl's. I wouldn't mind if you had a right face. I don't know what sort of faceen you have, a pale shrunken thingeen.' She turned to Grandma. 'Eat up.'

Her own face was pale, and bitter. She had been up all night. Strange to think Grandma was still eighty years older than I was. Her pulse, jutting out from her white wrist, beat slow and steady as the clock; she fell asleep again.

'Doctor Waldron said she's a heart like a man's. It's the arteries; the blood's not getting up to the head any more.' Margaret's face softened. She talked as if Grandma was already dead. 'Weren't they the great people? But, sure, what did they do only work and pray?'

'I'll go for a walk before it's dark.'

'Do. And lock up the hens.' She switched on the light—the ESB had come finally—a converted standard lamp, brass bowl still slop-slopping oil dregs as she moved it so it would not shine in Grandma's eyes.

In the flash of winter evening sun, the magpie's nest in the sycamores flung a shadow as big as a barrel across the opposite hillside. A bit like an otter's bite was gone from the fish back hill. Down through it came a soft low wind making a Shh-shh-shh like a broom across the land. There were not even cattle in the fields now, never mind people. The sandpits were still going, but Brod had gone to England. His father's trees were so tall now, you could not see the smoke from his chimney, but my father's lines of Lombardy poplars were dying, pencil-straight olive trunks rotting under skins of moss.

Sleugh . . . sleugh . . . . Each step I sank to my ankles. What was I doing down here when Mary Cole had not only sent me a Christmas card but, of all things, had telephoned me, talked with me last night for half-an-hour? And first thing this morning I had taken the train down here.

Sleugh . . . sleugh . . . . Even the ditch—I lay back to watch a skein of wild geese go crying overhead—was sopping. Underwater, the bottom fields were luminous yellow-green. Water bubbling up everywhere, cutting the bog into scraws, tiny islands of acid turf sheening the water with a beautiful rainbow slick as it trickled down to the river, itself as weedy as the fields.

Sleugh . . . sleugh . . . . and up came, not a duck flying for its life from my new twelve bore, but an otter! His shining eyes looked at me for just long enough for mine to take him in—white breast and short whiskers—and then he sank down again. Year after year I had been coming down here and had never seen one. It was as if he knew the place was deserted now.

Up again, fifty yards downstream, ducked down again and a V of rippling silkweed ran back towards me. Up again! right at my feet, gliding into a bed of reeds—or was it the bank?—watching me watching.

That was one good thing about a gun. With it, you could stand around for ever and no-one passed any remark. Without it, I had been taken for a Jehovah's Witness.

Tss-ss! He wanted to play! He slid underwater again, glided on his back to the surface and began chewing a reed with enormous noise. Like me on St Stephen's night, when Mr Cole smiled and drew the door shut, leaving us alone—Mary Cole and me together on a deep couch with globe glasses of brandy and biscuits. Crunch-crunch . . . closer closer . . . and then suddenly we were talking about Pax Romana.

The otter slipped suddenly out of sight and I heard the noise of the train, the boat train, appearing out of a frosty red west, blowing a blast of the horn as it rattled over the bridge; packed, blazing with lights, the bar carriage at the end trailing the sound of singing.

'Hi!'

A cloud of smoke and through it appeared John Edward! He was burning furze, burning everything in fact. He lit a cigarette, tossed the match lightly onto a ditch and bracken, blackthorn, furze, all burst into flames.

'You're welcome home. How're you going on?'

'I've just seen a—' instead of otter, I said 'water-dog', but still my voice sounded paper thin beside his.

'Did you get him?' He took my gun to examine.

'It's new.'

'It's awful heavy.' He fired at a thrush, singing a scrap of its spring song and handed it back to me. The report died slowly away as the thrush fell down through the branches. 'Come here—did you hear Hannah's getting married?'

I had an excited feeling, then I had not. 'I thought she was going to be a nun?'

'Urrah! she left that! He's an Irishman but . . . .'

He took another cigarette, lit it for me, laid the match in another mountain of furze. He smiled—he had got new, false teeth. 'A pity it's not a stickeen of dynamite!' He went back up the hill, turning to call back, 'Come on back tonight, can't you? We're going gaffing salmon.'

Sleugh . . . sleugh . . . . Every bird for a mile could hear me. A cock pheasant flew up far ahead, a rattle of wings flashing like armour, a mighty crow, 'The lord's bird,' Grandma called him, said I was not to shoot him. I fired and the pheasant crowed again, gliding on set wings for a quarter of a mile across bog and river, stepping proudly through the frosty scutch grass into another furzey ditch.

'Hi! Stop the bleddy noise!'

John Edward hammered the salmon spear again. His mother shouted from the house again, 'Hi! Don't you know Father Eamon is home?'

That was for me. I put my hands in my pockets as John Edward banged the last barb flat and a jet of sparks went into the dark.

'On my solemn! If I get out to ye!'

'Rub the snots off now and we're right.' he took a file and got to work on the barb points. We were in his father's forge, a turf shed now that his father was in England, with warm black sods up to the neck of the anvil, up to the rafters at the back. John Edward had not grown tall, but he was strong. I tried to hold the spear flat on the anvil, but each stroke of his file sent it sliding. Slowly, out of rusty points as stained and blunted as his fingers, four silvery tips appeared. 'Twas an old car spring.' He tested them on his stubbled jaw.

173

'From Mannion's old car,' John Patrick said. He was coming too, Hannah's half-brother. 'The old Anglia—IZ 987.'

' Twasn't then. Twas Grogan's Skoda—IZ 346.'

'How're ye men!' Father Eamon crept in from the dark, invisible in his clerical black. He was not a priest yet, but would be if his mother had her way.

'How's Maynooth?'

'God, do you think will I stick it?' He lit a cigarette. 'How's Uni?'

'Are ye college boys coming or not?' John Edward soused a sod of turf in TVO, stolen from the sandpit tank.

'Father Eamon!' his mother screamed through the dark. 'You'll be doing your priesting above in Mountjoy!'

He went slowly back inside and we went up a muddy boreen, talking of what we would do if we met the bailiff. That was a thought—together again with Alo in jail. The boreen ran out into grass, pitch black until we passed old Mannion's gable where a crack of light showed. John Edward pressed an eye to the broken chimney wall, we pressed behind him and saw, through flames and smoke, old Mannion going to bed, lying down with a whimper on a heap of sacks and overcoats on the hearthstone.

Sleugh . . . sleugh . . . . We came to the top of the hill and saw Orion stalking out before us, vanishing as we went down the far side and set a match to the dripping sod. The whole back of the hill lit up, black smoke pouring up into the sky.

'Lads! Lads!' Father Eamon crashed over a ditch and appeared in the blaze light.

'We'll all be blessed tonight.' John Edward held the light out over the water and, almost at once, a shape, silvery white as the stars, appeared. Father Eamon leaned over. I held his coat-tail.

'That's the Pay. We do leave the pay alone.'

'There's the Camóg!'

Just behind the hen fish, maybe waiting to milt her eggs, the big black neb of the cock fish glided into the light. Father Eamon rose on his toes, plunged the spear, but the fish twisted and vanished.

'Christ, you're one clumsy priest! Give me here.' John Edward took the spear.

A duck flew up quacking, a curlew cried and we heard an aeroplane far away. We came to the noisy water and speared a trout. In the water and on the end of the spear she looked small, but on the bank she was a fine fish—until a pint of spawn poured out of the hole in her side.

The drops of burning oil hummed as they dropped to the water. Another salmon cruised into the blaze, his tail drifting from side to side as he followed the light closer, closer to the bank. John Edward drove down suddenly on the handle of the spear and there was a white seethe of water. I thought of the grilse I had caught in my hands in Renvyle long ago. But this was not any young fish nervous in the estuary for the first time. It was a big, big as a pig, cock salmon who must have been making his way up year by year, maybe ever since I had first come down here, up the tangle of rivers and streams that led to this bed of gravel. Home.

'Come up, you pleb!' John Edward caught the long handle low down the haft as it it was a slane and—a sucking tearing noise—tossed the salmon like a slab of turf high up the bank. His blood shone black in the blaze. My blood thrilled. When I got back to Dublin—here, now, for the first time, I could actually imagine it—I would *kiss* her. Mary Cole.

In another half-hour we were finished. Two salmon and a trout. Sla-sla. It was freezing hard now. We walked back to John Patrick's house to avoid Father Eamon's mother. Cassiopeia hung over it, upside down like a giant M. In the high moonlight,

against the frozen fields, the white thatch and sparkling white-
wash were invisible. It was all as pale blank as the back of
Joseph's painting. Only the scent of turf smoke to say that here
was . . . .

'Hi! Hold on—' Father Eamon crept to the door and listened
and we heard then the litany of the rosary carry out into the icy
stillness.

'Mystical Rose.'

'Pray for us.'

'Tower of David.'

'Pray for us.'

'Tower of ivory.'

'Pray for us.'

'House of gold.'

'Pray for us.'

'There's a dropeen left yet.' John Edward lit the sod again
and we trailed after him as, with sudden random energy, he
began combing the garden hedge for birds. A bullfinch, his head
under his wing, his rose breast fluffed out for the night. A
blackbird—his bright yellow eye blinked awake, too late. A
missle thrush in the ivy beard of the hawthorn tree. His fury was
catching; we helped him wring their necks.

'Will you ever forget the time you shot me!' John Edward
brushed a cowlick back off his forehead. 'Haven't I the mark of
it yet. Here!' He tossed me the blackbird. 'You'd a right to give
that to old Mrs Kenny. They reckon there's a cure in the soup.'

I felt the last flutter as I warmed my numb fingers in his
feathers; then he lay still in my pocket.

'God Almighty! They're still at it.'

'And three Hail Marys for Hannah in Hammersmith . . . .'

'And this day fortnight, please God—' John Edward held the
last flames of the sod up under the eaves until the thatch caught
fire'—I'll be over there myself.'

'Are you going?' I said. 'Doing what?'

'The building.'

'Hi! Do not!' John Patrick beat out the little blaze with the flat of the spear. I had not heard that John Edward was leaving. I had a lonely feeling, even as we heard the scrape of chairs and we went inside, even as we ate supper—sweet tea and Hannah's stepmother's boxty cake. We left the fish in the cow house. As John Edward said, they were red rotten.

18

DUNLOP FOOTWEAR DIARY 1964

January 8   Grandma sleeping. walkd out to see Petie. Not home. Margaret jaded. Left for Dublin. Card from Browne.

January 11   Mary C. came up to me in the library. Couldn't think of anything to say. She went away. *I just couldn't speak.*

January 14   Telegram from Margaret. Grandma un – conscious.

January 15   Grandma died.

January 20   Snow. Dada ordered logs.

February 1   Aunt Josie sent *Tatler* photo of Sean. Dada splitting logs.

February 28   Heavy snow. Saw Gorman with Mary Cole. Holding hands.

March 5   Roger asked Roderick and me to stay for the holidays.

******

The first thing I saw in England was a huge photo of Harold

Macmillan, peeling off a hoarding that covered the gable end of a house. Under his crinkled smiling moustache were the words 'You've Never Had It So Good." It was daybreak and we were coming into Huddersfield. I felt another jump of excitement in my stomach. (The first had been in Holyhead, as we came down the gangplank in the dark, when I saw a policeman familiar from a hundred films smiling from under his helmet brim as he scanned our faces.) It was the words. I was used to Irish signs with the words in two languages, and now there was only one. Huddersfield had never been, was not anything else. You've Never Had It So Good would never be translated into any other language. It seemed too real to be true and I looked automatically to see what was 'behind'. But there was no 'behind'. It made everything seem larger than life, super real like Macmillan's face on the house gable. Roderick was at home here, so was Roger, so was Harold Macmillan, so was the man sitting opposite in our horsebox carriage. I had never seen anything like him. He looked as if he had stepped off a film set: flat check cap, dirty white short wool scarf knotted like a cravat, smoking a dirty white short clay pipe, reading *The Daily Worker* ; on the seat beside him, a tin lunchbox, its corners worn shiny.

'Slag and fog!' Roger rattled open *The Times* he had bought at Holyhead, as if to shut off the view. Instead of making me jump less, his accent here made me jump more. I looked at the man opposite, but he did not seem to notice us.

The train stopped, the man said 'Ta-ra' and got out. A woman in blue serge trousers, her hair dyed blonde, was sweeping the platform. She shouted something at the man, he shouted back. Their voices reminded me of Austin.

'Do we go through Castleford?'

'No, actually,' Roger said. 'Thank God.'

Actually I was not very interested in seeing where Austin lived, anymore than he was interested in me. Actually, at

Grandma's funeral, he had spent more time talking to John Edward than to me. Actually, they had gone back together on the same train.

Now we were going through Leeds, where Brod was, and out into green farming country that grew white with snow as we climbed. 'More like it,' Roderick said. 'Reminds me of Austria.'

Roger put down *The Times*. 'What were you doing there anyhow?'

'Studying, sport!'

'Studying what?'

'Philosophy,' Roderick said. 'I packed it in. In the end, I was just lying in bed.'

'How long were you there?' It was a question I had long wanted to ask.

'Four years.'

'My God,' Roger said. 'How old are you?'

'Twenty-three.'

Five years older than us, yet when he took up *The Times* and began reading bits aloud—'Jack Ruby on Death Row for Oswald killing'—and Roger drawled, 'Oh, do shut up', he shut up.

The train emptied, filled gradually again. Two boys on their way to school sat opposite, talking about their father's farms.

'We ga tew ton th'acre th' knowest.'

'Tha were a'reet!'

They were The Archers. Then a man actually wearing a bowler hat began talking to me. He was Richard Wattis. My voice wobbled the way it did when I was cycling and a bus brushed by. Two soldiers got on, their kitbags and arms tattooed with the names of girls and foreign cities. When I noticed on one of their cigarette packets, the word 'knickers', written in big illiterate block capitals, I was creepily fascinated and could not look away. They began playing poker, slamming down the cards on each others' thighs. They joked with the ticket collector when he came in, and he joked with the man in the bowler, who joked with the two farming schoolboys. I kept quiet. If Cuchulain, Daniel O'Connell and Patrick Pearse crept out from under my seat, I was ready to cut them dead rather than risk a frown from this red-cheeked man in the blue-peaked cap, smiling at me as he handed me back my punched ticket.

Still climbing, the snow deeper now, each farm prettier than the last. Down then to a town. 'Reminds me a bit of Sligo. I used to go there when I was a kid. I remember my grandfather used to put a lump of butter in his porridge—' Roderick broke off— 'Hey, is that a *cathedral?*'

'Ripon.'

Roderick wiped the window and gazed out. I was beginning to see why I liked him. 'That's the great thing about Gothic architecture . . . .' He was off again, talking about The Western Tradition. ' . . . the decoration is part of the structure.'

'What else could it be part of?' Roger snapped. The nearer we got to his home, the more irritable he became.

'Well, it could just be stuck on.'

'Like your hat?'

That was what life in their flat was like, according to Gorman. He dropped in there some nights—on his way home from Mary Cole's, I guessed.

The snow—it was not like Mayo snow—lay like cotton wool on the boughs of oak trees the colour of iron. Even Roger's father's car, a sporty red Triumph, seemed more at home here, like the snow-thatched red pillar box outside the station door.

'Pater!'

Roger actually called his father 'Pater' and, when he asked how his mother was, he called her 'Mater'. Dr Murphy said Mater was marvellous. Everything was marvellous to me as we drove through silent white smoking villages as clear-cut as the briar pipe Dr Murphy held clenched-cocked between his teeth.

He talked of the latest local murder, a *crime passionel,* he said, until a huge ruin appeared through trees, a soft gold against the snow. Fountains Abbey, Roger said, and we turned up a little drive to a big square house made of the same soft yellow stone. At the back door, a girl with hair the same colour was unharnessing a horse the colour of the snow.

'This is Upper something,' Roderick muttered in my ear.

'Can't beat old England, eh?' he said to me when we were alone. We were sharing a bedroom, its ceiling glittering in the snowy light, its floor dark from the lead sky. 'Christ!' His mood changed as suddenly. 'Dead beats, on the run . . . . ' He pointed out at a man and a woman in tweed, striding across the snow after two big bounding dogs. 'Wilful innocence—that's the whole English thing, you know.' He unpacked his suitcase—dressing gown, travelling clock, Burckhardt's *Renaissance*—huge, but packed to the brim. And always would be, even then I knew. Roderick's Grand Ideal, which kept reality at arm's length, would gobble up everything—gothic cathedrals, Sligo butter, the classical tradition, all piled without distinction, like grist outside the fairy mill to be ground into purest fare some day . . . some day . . . .

'And how did you fellows meet?' Brogues set wide apart on the fender, Dr Murphy swayed before a log fire? 'All doing Law?'

'Nope!' Roderick filled his new pipe from his new pouch, offered some to Dr Murphy ('Four Square—it's the real thing') and talked about thirteenth century Europe until his matchbox was empty. Then a maid came in. I did not understand a single word she said.

'The old daily round!' Dr Murphy tapped his pipe out on his heel.

'My old man was a doc too,' Roderick said. 'He's packed it in now.'

Past the breakfast-room window, racehorses slender as deer walked single file, small stable hands sitting high up their shoulders like cardboard cut-outs. Roger's mother came in, welcomed us and took away a vase of brown beech sprays. His sister played the piano in another room. When we went for a walk, even the silence seemed different. It was my first time out of Ireland.

'What do you think?' Roger's pale blonde face brightened as we approached the gold skeleton of Fountains Abbey.

'Cistercians, were they? Amazing.' Roderick followed in his Chelsea boots, a newspaper he had taken from the hall table sticking out of his pocket. 'Those guys knew their stuff. Mmm! Look at that window.'

'There's a staircase here you can—'

'No thanks, sport. You go on. I'll sit here.' His voice followed us as we toured the ruins. Cellarium . . . cloister garth . . . . Roger knew every door and stairs as if he lived there. 'Chee-hee-hee.' I heard the *Beano* laugh as I looked through what Roger said was a leper's squinch. Visitors' rooms . . . refectory . . . mill. It was like a little city. High up on a tower looking across the white landscape, we heard Roderick's voice again, reading aloud from the newspaper far below:

'"Richard Burton and Elizabeth Taylor were married in Montreal yesterday. Mr Burton said 'I am very happy.' Mrs Burton declined to comment." Chee-hee-hee!'

'Christ!' Roger said and, as it began to snow again—'Let's go home.'

Roderick knew how to make himself at home; he even had a

183

second bath that evening. At dinner—second helpings—he left Burckhardt on the sideplate. In the drawing room afterwards, he remarked on the pictures, then drew in to the fire. Dr Murphy brought out the whiskey—Powers—all at once talking about Dublin.

'The old Bailey still there? Marvellous old place!'

'They're doing it up.' I said, 'actually.'

'The old fire down at the end! Lovely old place Dublin then. But never go back—that's what they say.' He threw back his whiskey, poured us each a glass and another for himself and sat, resting his brogues on the fireplace. 'Must be forty years ago, I remember going in there one morning—the old Bailey. Not a sinner only myself—' His voice slipped into a Cork accent. He sipped some whiskey, rested his shoes higher up the fireplace. 'Not a sinner only myself. Then, in walks Gogarty, Oliver St John Gogarty.'

Roger said, 'The writer, Pater?'

'Writer, poet, surgeon, statesman, wit.'

'Bit of an athlete too, wasn't he?' Roderick settled in his chair.

'But to make a long story short, wasn't I reading the paper—the old *Irish Times* still going? Marvellous paper! And a photo of de Valera on the front page. And I said to myself, I'll just . .' Dr Murphy slid the bottle as once the paper across the table. 'Well, his face!' Dr Murphy's face turned a convincing shade of purple. "*Mais ou est le nez Danton?*'" he said, quick as a flash. "*Mais ou est le nez Danton!*"' Dr Murphy drew back the bottle. 'Of course, you simply don't get characters like that anymore.' He crossed his ankles, tapped under the mantel with his toes. 'Old Dicky Muldowney still going? Chest man. Went to Surgeons together. "My God, Paddy," he'd say to me. "My God, Paddy, you're a terrible man." Used to go racing together. Clonmel, Limerick . . . .'

Roger's mother came in with a vase of just opened dafffodils and set them on the baby grand and said she was going to bed. Dr Murphy smiled even more and poured us each a stiff one, a stiffer one for himself and rested his heels on the mantelpiece. He seemed to be standing almost on his head.

'Nelson's Pillar still there? Wonder they haven't blown it up! Probably think it's a phallic symbol.'

Roger stared silently into the fire.

'Doric, isn't it?' Roderick was off again.

'A Doric cock!' Dr Murphy began, but then Roger's sister came in , sat down and began talking about school. She went to the Sacred Heart and we chatted about that. Dr Murphy waggled his shoes and stared up at them in silence. Another drink and he interrupted suddenly—'Bloody things! Where do they come from?'

'What's this, Pater?'

'More interestingly,' Dr Murphy threw back his drink. 'Where do they go to?'

'Not with you,' Roderick said.

'*What happens to old Sacred Heart pictures?*' He tapped the frame of the Adam mirror impatiently with a toe.

'Expect they end up in junk shops.'

'And then?'

'I suppose people buy them,' Roderick went on. 'For the frame, or something.'

'All right,' Dr Murphy nodded, thinking as he poured another whiskey. 'And then?'

'They probably put their own picture in the frame. You know, a Medici print . . . .'

'The PICTURE! What happens to that? They don't just vanish, you know!'

'Give up.'

'I'll tell you.' Dr Murphy tipped the last of the bottle into his glass and roared suddenly with laughter. 'They *burn* them!'

185

'Never thought of that, Doc.'

'Chee-hee-hee!' Upstairs, when we were alone, Roderick laughed his *Beano* laugh until I was laughing too. 'Chee-hee-hee!'

DUNLOP FOOTWEAR DIARY 1964

March 16   Roger in bed. Bad cold, Mrs Murphy said.
              (Seems to like me—asked how much longer I
              can stay.) Great chat with Dr Murphy. Mar-
              vellous character. 2 sherry. 3 wine. 4 whiskey.

March 17   Roger still in bed. Dr Murphy marvellous
              form. Said to stay as long as we like.

March 18   Roger up again. Suggested we go to his aunt's
              house in Westmoreland. Roderick left for
              Derbyshire (home).

So I was going west again. Now Roger was driving the sporty red Triumph. I lay back in the bucket seat and watched the white road shooting underneath. There were only the two of us. At the last moment, Roderick had decided to go home and collect some books.

'Books! He practically looks like a book! Actually, Mater said she thought he was rather brainless. And when he *is* reading, did you notice he has a lazy eye? wandering all over the place—half the time I think he's looking at me. I say, do you think he's queer?'

Roger was doing over sixty miles an hour. I got nervous as

he glanced from the road to me. He lit a cigarette. Half-a-dozen drags and the red tip was an inch from his lips. I looked out the window, because I liked Roger, but I liked Roderick too. In a way, they were like two sides of a coin. Like that penny Mary Cole and I had held between our foreheads at Browne's party— which seemed suddenly so long ago. The speedometer needle had turned seventy now. We passed another signpost; I had never seen so many.

'Where's this?' I tried to change the subject. 'Westmorland?'

'West-more-land! Christ, can't you say it properly? "Westmorland!"' He shot through another crossroads at seventy-five. 'What sort of fucking accent is that anyhow?' He pronounced it 'focking'.

'Neutral,' I ventured.

'Oh fuck! There's no such fucking thing.' His face was paler than his blonde hair. He went down to third gear, took a snow-banked bend at fifty; in a minute he was up to eighty again, eighty-five, ninety, touching a hundred on the snow-packed motorway to Kendal. The Triumph began to shudder. So did I. I said, 'Slow focking down', but he went even faster, until I was too frightened to speak.

I tried often to remember the rest of that drive, but could not, any more than I could remember the rest of that evening long ago with Jennifer in the linen cupboard. But like the hotel soap scent, I thought was her scent, fright afterwards brought it back to me.

I thought of it a few months later when I heard of Roger's father's death; and again, much later, when I heard that it was suicide. I thought of it again next summer when I went with Roderick on holidays to Heidelberg, when he announced after just one night, as suddenly as he had announced that he was going home to Derbyshire, that he was heading off on his own to Italy to see the Byzantine mosaics. And, again, one night after a dance—old Belvedere— when the lights came on and a woman went up on the stage, blinking in the spotlight dazzle, and I recognised Judy, so fat and bloated I thought at first she must be pregnant, until I saw one of the band grin and hand her a pint of lager. And yet it came up clearest, clear as a photograph, the year after, when O'Hara and Gorman and I went to Greece—the one holiday we ever spent together. We were in Athens, on the Acropolis, of course, O'Hara and I lying under the Erecththeum in the shade, smoking as we watched Gorman out in the heat going from column to column of the Parthenon, guidebook in hand. It was Gorman who did everything: got us up early in the mornings, hitched the lift, sat in front with the driver making conversation, carried the big rucksack with maps and the 'field dressing' his father had given us in case of accident. He must have made us feel guilty, for we got up and had a look at the Caryatids—soon, according to a guide we eavesdropped on, to be taken into the museum and replaced by copies. As we walked over to join Gorman, O'Hara said, 'Did I tell you I've given up Architecture?'

'For what?'

'Law.' He flicked away his cigarette end.

I forget how we began talking about Mary Cole, Gorman and I, as we wandered through the rubble—possibly O'Hara's saying one of the Caryatids looked a bit like her.

He was still going out with her—two, three, four evenings a week and having lunch with her family on Sunday.

'Are you sure you're still not interested in her?' Gorman looked at me.

I said 'No', must have said it quite loudly because O'Hara turned around. And then Gorman said—strange, he used the same words his father had that day he asked if we had put stones in our snowballs, when we shook our heads: *I believe you.*

I remembered then for some reason as we walked down the

hill together, not just that terrifying drive across the Pennines, but the heavenly relief as we shot over the ridge of the last hill and Roger drawled, 'Here we are,' and took his foot off the accelerator and we coasted forty miles an hour through a pretty village, thirty, twenty, ten and turned in gates to an old house, varnished over with virginia creeper, an old English sheepdog saying Woof-woof at the door, but a bit—it struck me—like Margaret's, the same bare long view through wind-burned sycamores at the back.

DUNLOP FOOTWEAR DIARY 1964

March 19   Snowing like blazes. Red Lion. Marvellous old pub (15th century). Roger drunk. Played rings. Said he'd once spent the night out on his bedroom windowsill hiding from his father. Threw rings in fire. (Inglenook 14th century). Thrown out.

March 21   Wish I hadn't to go back. No one wanted me to really. Mrs Murphy drove me to station. Met Roderick at Holyhead. New hat. No books. Seemed sad. Said mother slammed door in his face. Said parents are separated. Since he was ten. Said mother walked out one morning & never came back. Talked all the way to Dublin. Said he'd been in Jesuits (Austria). Sick. Home.

IV

FATHER MACNAMARA

19

'You're all right for cash?' my father said quickly around the study door, in the same way he had said, only a few years before, 'Now you're clear about *sex*?'.

'Yes, yes.'

'Dada—'

'ONE MINUTE!'

My mother went quickly back into the kitchen.

'It'll be an experience . . . .' He held out his hand. 'You might telephone from New York?'

'Okey doke.'

Touched my hand, turned away. 'WHAT IS IT, MAMA?'

'If you're going to Grange . . . I want *fresh* eggs from Mrs Casey . . . .'

A rattle of golf sticks in the hall, the hall door slammed, the grey hump-back Rover roof slid out of sight and I went into the breakfast room. Tucked under my side plate—a coloured wad of bank notes, tightly rubber-banded. I was going to America.

'Glad you decided to take the plunge,' Father MacNamara had written. I still had his precise, black ink letter in my pocket, re-reading it on the way to the airport. '. . . Americans believe, by and large, that most human problems can be defeated by hard work and imagination; they may be wrong, but they have fun in the process . . . .' He still used a Greek 'e'.

'You go on—'

'No, I'll see you off.' My brother rooted through a jumble of invoice sheets on the dashboard—he was in the business now— and took out a book, *Diverse Ways to Tackle Trout*, and sat reading by the Departures window until I had vanished up a tunnel into the great plane's belly.

I had my own reading, my novel. I had written a novel—nearly. The hero was dead, buried alive in Mayo, but some closing chapters still lay ahead. The manuscript was in my briefcase under my seat and, as we flew across an arctic snowscape of pure cloud, fresh developments kept occurring. I kept taking it out, writing in the margins . . . . 'Then the moon appeared behind the sycamores like a monstrance through a roodscreen . . .'

I was so busy with this that it wasn't until New York appeared underneath that it dawned on me: I was bound for the United States, sure as the 12 bus went to the Pillar.

Noon. And I had left Dublin at noon. A strange sense of stepping outside time.

'You an actor!'

'No, actually.'

The Customs man looked at my passport and then again at my suitcase, tossing my new tropical linen jacket, lifting up the large wooden crucifix, a gift from Father Bodkin, the briar pipe almost as big as Roderick had presented when he went back to England and then the cut-throat razor Petie had sharpened up and given me.

'Reckon he'd cut the mustard?' he said to the other Customs man and they both laughed. I didn't.

'You *Irish*?'

'Yes, actually.'

'Actually, could you open that briefcase.'

He pulled out my precious folder, flicked through the foolscap pages, packed it back again, yawning 'Next' to the man behind me.

Behind glass doors, I could see my Aunt Rita and her friend,

Bess, waving to me. They had a porter waiting.

'This boy has come all the way from Ireland,' they said as he wheeled my case to a taxi. They said it again to the taxi driver.

'Get right back there—' and did not speak until we were in Manhattan. 'All the rats come out at night—' he slid back his partition as we drove through Time Square. 'And the mice.'

I dragged my eyes from girls lining the kerbs, from pink cinema titles and magazine shops, up to a high screen flashing news in letters ten feet tall—'Pope Paul has urinary tract.'

'I bet you never have a bit of trouble,' my Aunt Rita said.

'You're goddam right, lady.' He reached under his seat and took out an iron bar.

'An odd ball,' Aunt Rita said. She and Bess had lived together for thirty years in this tiny pink-and-gilt flat high above Lexington Avenue. From their double-glazed window, the city below seemed as remote as their colour television playing in the corner, the sound turned down. Together in the minute kitchen, they squeezed past each other as they prepared cocktails. Together in the bedroom, they changed for dinner. It crossed my mind that maybe they were ... different. In fact, when Rita said later that evening, 'No, I never liked my father,' when I noticed the ruby on Bess's wedding finger, my hopes rose sensationally. I should have known, I thought, when Rita told me of Bess's fiancé's death. What did I expect with a Sacred Heart picture above the fridge in the Manhattan kitchen?

'This boy has come all the way from Ireland,' Bess told the taxi driver as we drove to dinner, told the waiter as he led her to a table well away from the Jews and Niggers she saw everywhere. She talked in her deep New York voice about the good old days, when the girls stood waiting for their young men with hands a little raised so the blood ran back and left them snow white. My Aunt Rita did all the listening, her head cocked, cynical expression wrinkling her big nose. It was like looking at

193

my grandmother, my father, or—I glanced at my reflection in the mirror—myself. A mention of home moved Rita from listener to talker and I heard suddenly that her mother had been in America as a girl. I was amazed. My grandmother, the root of our enormous family, in whose house I was burying my novel's hero, had lived here. It was like seeing a fuchsia bush appear outside in 5th Avenue.

'Where?'

'Philadelphia. All the Flynns went to Philly. Nell got a job as a companion to a Miss Penfield, a millionaire. She loved Nell, threw money at her. That's how Nell bought Knockshinny. She bought it as a summer house . . . .'

I drank it all down with the icy cocktails Rita set before me and afterwards, head swimming, wrote it all down in my diary—that grew nearly as long as my novel. I could not leave out a single detail, any more than leave unopened one of those magazines with bare-breasted goddesses on the covers, smiling down at me from top shelves.

'Who's going to meet him in Knoxville?' Bess fussed the next morning.

'He'll meet himself.' Forty years out of Ireland and Rita still had a voice like hawthorn.

Each, when the other was not looking, slipped a ten dollar bill into a pocket of my charcoal suit and away I went on a Greyhound bus, umbrella, pipe, crucifix and all. All night their divan had vibrated under me like the aeroplane and soon I was asleep again, dazed by the straight carpet of asphalt rolling ahead. It was dark when the hilly roads of Tennessee woke me, the sky bright with neon signs: Little Chef, First Church of Christ Scientist, Burger King, Second Church of Christ Carpenter . . . thicker and faster as we came to Knoxville at last. That night my bed rose and fell under me like the bus seat. Next morning it was the lift. Up up up in my tropical linen jacket, I flew to the eleventh floor of the Arts Tower and stepped dizzy into an office made entirely of window. The History faculty were standing about, all about seven feet tall, raising paper cups of coffee to lips high above my head. One of them glanced down at the old pigskin briefcase O'Hara had given me as a going-away present, 'Hey, the pony express just come in!'

20

'Mrs Storey, do you mind if I put a nail in the wall?'

'What's that, Mr Kinney?'

'Do you mind if I put up a crucifix?'

My landlady smiled uneasily. 'How big is it, Mr Kinney?' — relaxing when she saw it— 'my husband, why he was a Catholic too' —taking me down the hallway into her dark, cluttered bedroom, showing me his photo on the wall in a birdseye maple frame. 'Used to go to church too . . . .' She drew a hammer from her dressing-table drawer. 'There, hammer just as many nails as you like, Mr Kinney.'

'No, no! Just one, Mrs Storey.'

The elation of those first autumn months in Tennessee: Home four thousand miles away, my novel about home four feet away on the bedside table. It was so hot I slept naked, an extraordinary sensation: some mornings when I threw back the sheet and felt the warm air on my skin, it seemed I might lift off the bed and float. From the railway, the squeal of wheels, the snap of points changing. Windows wide open behind zinc gauze screens. Our Father . . . shave . . . . Then coffee and flapjacks with maple syrup waiting for me on Mrs Storey's potbelly stove. She had taken a shine to me.

'You come on back this evening—I'm making hominy grits.' She followed me onto the flaking white veranda and saw me down the steps, saw a black man go whistling by and turned back abruptly inside—'Them darn nigroes, lowering the tone o' this street . . . .'

Every week an electric storm ending in a cloudburst that

washed the red clay out of her garden down onto the path. Baked dry the next day, swept back the next, and the following week washed out again. Cardinals birds and squirrels in the magnolias . . . bird-sized private planes, green, red, buzzing in and out of town just above the rooftops . . . black drunks sitting on one kerb, white evangelists shouting about St Paul on the other . . . . The wonderful *difference* of it all, I reflected as I darted in the door of McClung Tower. I pressed the Call button and a lift came rushing down its innards.

Professor Graf was head of the History Department, Leroy P. Graf. We sat in a horseshoe around him as he explained our duties. Through a window, I could see the big blue horseshoe of the Smokey Mountains. There were a dozen of us, Graduate Assistants—one for each professor and lecturer, for whom we would mark freshman papers, proctor exams, grade scripts, leaving the rest of our time our own to attend seminars, write term papers, do research for our theses.

I looked at my watch: ten past ten . . . ten past five in Ireland. Professor Graf looked at me, then at his own watch. I almost heard the click! as his dislike for me began. I listened carefully again.

'Over and above all this, I will be meeting you here, Room 1108, each Monday at 4.00 p.m. to give a special class on Historical Method.' He smiled. 'Now, let's get to know each other.'

He was a graduate of Harvard. He was married. Due to the fact that Mrs Graf and he had married quite late in life, they had a family of young children: a boy of twelve and a girl of nine. His introductory sketch of himself lasted five minutes and, in that time, I realised that I was not going to be a historian. I had always known that, but it had been nice to dream otherwise, especially when it meant getting out of Ireland. Now, Professor Graf's academic voice rang through me like an alarm clock. I had one academic year to go—less five minutes . . . ten . . . . He was

197

working his way around the horseshoe.

A girl sitting opposite me began taking notes, crossing and uncrossing long sun-tanned legs, stopping only when Professor Graf asked for her sketch of herself. She had taken a B.A. last summer, majoring in Western Civ. and Black Literature. A boy called Bill Jackson was aiming at a Ph.D. on Andrew Jackson.

A middle-aged woman in boots and jeans listed all the graduate programmes she had taken, going back to the very year I was born.

'Do we call you—' Professor Graf looked at the sheet of paper before him —'Adrian or Kenny?'

'Either, Mr Graf.'

The woman in jeans said, 'What kind of name is that?'

'Which?'

Sherry, the girl with the brown legs, laughed. Professor Graf smiled his frosty New England smile. I noticed later that he had a huge loving knowledge of England—he treated the sole English graduate in our group as if he was a prize marrow—and a corresponding blank for Ireland. Maybe he thought Kenny was another first name? that in Ireland we did not use second names? Anyhow, he called me Kenny after that, even after I had taken Bill's advice and begun to call him 'Professor.'

'You did all right, Kenny,' Sherry said afterwards. 'You too, Bill.'

'You reckon?' Bill scrubbed his eyes.

We were in a bar he had found—at the end of my street, it turned out. Tennessee was a dry state, Bill explained, but you could always find someplace: the police winked at it because only the blacks drank there.

'Ain't too many coons here though.' He blinked and looked around. The shack was full of white faces familiar already from the big roomy lift going up and down McClung Tower. The German who said 'Guten Tag' and got out at the Philosophy floor was crammed into a chair under a slot machine tv. Mr Craig, lecturer in nineteenth-century European history, was sitting at the sunny little window in a tilted back chair reading *Playboy*. Someone in working clothes swayed up to the tv and put in a quarter and I recognised him too—Charlie, another of Mrs Storey's lodgers.

'Jeez,' Bill said, 'I hate skin flicks.'

'What'll you have?' I produced Rita's ten dollar bill.

'Don't do it! Jeez, don't do it, baby!' Charlie raised an arm, shielding his eyes as the striptease began. Rapt, I hardly heard the voice alongside, calling me—what I had not heard since school, and that morning from Professor Graf— 'Kenny . . . .' Power detached himself super-slow from the bar and strolled across. He had been ahead of me at school. I had heard he was here.

'Jesus—this is too much. What took you down here?'

'History.'

'You're in McClung, huh?'

I tried an 'uh-huh'. 'What are you up to?'

'Did my doctorate last fall. Lecturing now.' He bit the end off a green cigar. 'Economics.' He lit the other end.

'And you got married too?' He had a wedding ring.

He unbent a bit. 'Just had a kid.' He smiled. 'Beverley.'

'Congratulations. A boy?'

'A girl, for God's sake. *Beverley*. Dympna had enough of those Irish names.' He blew some smoke. 'Remember Kavanagh at school? His sister's here—married some mad dentist. They've just come down from—wait for it—Alaska!' He poured down half a can of beer, crushed the can. 'Be in touch!' Stubbed out nine-tenths of the green cigar. 'And we'll get together—OK?'

'OK.' I carried back three cans to Sherry and Bill. 'Hey! I've just met someone I know from Ireland.'

'Git!' Bill said. 'Watching that goddam stripper!'

199

At last it was evening and I was alone. Mrs Storey gave me a cup of coffee, disappointed that I did not take it with her by the potbelly stove. Alone in my room, I took out my typewriter and the folder only New York Immigration had seen. My novel.

The story was drifting. After the first hundred pages, I had lost my grip on the hero. The University of Tennessee's letter offering me a scholarship had just come in time and clinched the plot. A few chapters to show the hero's static Dublin life, and then, like me, he received a pale blue aerogramme from an American university. The last part was set in his aunt's house in Mayo where he went for a final summer holiday, where he would slowly disintegrate. Just as the day of departure for America was approaching, his aunt would fall mysteriously ill and he would stay on the pretext of nursing her, adamantly indifferent to his father's angry pleading. The plane would leave without him, his poor aunt would die, and he would rot away his life in Mayo. It was to be called *Patrick Fitzpatrick*.

I was flying towards those closing chapters now. I had them clear in my head: long purple passages that would bury Patrick in the sleep of oblivion . . . dozing by the river in the hot rushes, grasshoppers springing onto his clothes and off again . . . wandering in a warm mist by Mannin Lake, so warm he lay down again to doze in the heavy perfumed heather . . . . Tears came to my eyes, dissolving the words, as I hammered the keys, hammering him deeper and deeper into unconsciousness.

There was a knock at my door that made me jump six inches out of my chair. It was only Mrs Storey. 'You all right, Mr Kinney?'

'Grand. Grand!'

******

'"... Thus the word 'Protestantism' was a mere catchword, suitably emotive to attract the New England masses; suitably vague to attract the respectable; suitably ...."' Professor Graf paused and looked at me over my paper on 'The Historiography of the American Revolution'. I liked those semi-colons. He did not seem to like any of it. He gave his Woodrow Wilson smile and said 'Citations?'

'I put the citations together at the end, Professor.'

'I think we had agreed to sacrifice aesthetic appeal to the reader's convenience by putting citations at the foot of each page.' He turned to my last page.' '"Hilaire Belloc, *passim* "?'

'I looked at quite a few of his books, Professor.'

'I don't think they would be regarded as serious history this side of the Atlantic, Kenny.'

'I agree, Professor. They're awful! It's just that the library here has so many of them that I thought ....'

He dropped my paper onto the desk. His neatly pencilled 'Citations?' had been written over some longer comment he had erased. I should have known he was a serious Protestant. Before class, he chatted about the 'talks' they had at their Sunday services, on such matters as the religious beliefs of the Cherokee.

'Get that goddam Sherry shooting beavers,' Bill muttered.

'What's a "beaver", Bill?'

Professor Graf glanced sharply at me, then opened a folder and took out an immaculately typed lecture. He rested fingertips on the table. 'Today, I intend to talk about the use of italics ....'

Sherry crossed her bare legs, licked the tip of her pencil,

201

uncrossed her legs. I looked away, my mind following my gaze out of the window, wandering across the Smokey Mountains, turning from blue to fire red now as the leaves died, and down into the foothills, onto the shingle rooftops of the outskirts where I lived . . . where my novel lay. The question was—could I sustain . . . that was the word—could I *sustain* those last chapters of total collapse until my hero had sunk into . . . .

'—Italics, then, have not—I must repeat—have *not* the same function as the underlined word. Underlining denotes importance of material so underlined. Italicisation must be confined to quotations from a language other than the one one is writing in denoted by . . . .'

Sherry slipped a chewing gum pellet into her mouth as we went down in the lift, down down down. Her lips were lilac pink today. She blew a bubble, then another, as big as her breasts.

'What's your thesis on, Sherry?'

She burst the bubble with a bang, sucked the tatters back into her mouth. 'The Impact of Scots-Irish Railroad Workers on the Political Parties in Nineteenth Century East Tennessee. What's yourn?'

'Pre-Reformation Vernacular Sermons.'

'You got much stuff?'

'Not really, Sherry.'

'You coming for a Coke?'

'I ought to be going to the library.'

'Sure. That's where I'm going.'

The library had been built to look like an old English mansion, carefully covered with ivy, with carved stone windows and arched doors studded with huge black nail heads. Behind the Dewey Catalogue was the Western Civ. museum, locked always but the door was just iron bars so you could see all the paintings and statues and altarpieces inside—Madonnas and Crucifixions and saints in martyrdom.

'Jeez! It's scary. It's like a goddam church.' Sherry led the way through the turnstile and up the stairs to the bookstacks, avenues of giant green metal shelves. In my walks down these green glades, I had seen in the wastepaper bins sometimes empty bourbon bottles, once even a pair of woman's tights, but never a soul. Everyone lived in 'carrels', desks high-walled with more shelves, tucked away at the ends of avenues like woodland huts. Inside hers Sherry had pinned up photos. There were bottles of scent, make-up, and half-a-dozen bottles of Coke. She riffled through papers for a bottle opener, found a ring and put it on her wedding finger.

'Separated.' She found the bottle opener. 'I'm seeing Scott this afternoon. That's our little boy.' She snapped off the Coke caps. 'He likes to see the ring, I guess.'

'And were you married long?'

'Guess.'

How long?'

'A year.'

'That wasn't very long, Sherry, was it?'

'I guess when you're living with someone they don't seem that interesting—'

'SSSHHH!' came like a blackbird cry down a green avenue from some other woodland hut. I drank my Coke and Sherry said, 'You call by anytime, Kenny.'

Every book ever printed seemed to be in that colossal library. I pulled one out as I strolled down my avenue. Shakespeare, in antique padded leather binding, a woodcut plate inside—The Gift of Professor and Mrs Leroy P. Graf. A hundred volumes bound in blue: *The Spectator.Who's Who* 1900 . . . all the way to *Who's Who* 1967. A hundred thousand novels. Ten yards of poetry. Irish books too; some I had never heard of. *The Annals of Connaught*: . . . .'1422 A.D. . . . and after this Miles son of MacSiurtain Dubh was killed while in captivity in Mannin

Castle by Sefra son of Tomas Finn MacMuiris . . . .'

I gazed out of the mullioned windows. That was our
Mannin! And MacMuiris . . . We were related to the Fitzmaurices
too. Through the antique leaded panes I watched girls in short
orange skirts and white boots march past playing silver fifes.
Behind came a soldier standing in an open army car. General
Maxwell Taylor was going to make a recruiting speech for
Vietnam. I sat down and began a juicy passage for the last
chapter of my novel, flushing with excitement as I pushed my
hero deeper and deeper into the earth, day by day drawing
closer to the end.

On Friday nights you could almost hear the campus close down
for the weekend. Floor by floor from the top down, the lights
went out in McClung Tower. Then the unnatural silence like the
stillness before the electric storms. After dinner—on Fridays,
Mrs Storey fried me a big boney fish—we sat in the swing chair
on the veranda, watching the undergraduate cars go by, a
procession of white-walled tyres shining in the dusk, becoming
a procession of headlights going faster, the car radios playing
louder in the petrol-scented air. It was late when Sherry's green-
finned Chrysler glided to a stop by the light of the veranda.

'Youall have a real good time!' Mrs Storey beamed, watching us out of sight.

'Some car.'

'My Daddy gave it to me when I split from Bill.'

'Bill was your husband?'

'Uh-huh.' She smiled. Her lipstick seemed almost white
tonight. 'What do you think of him?'

'Have I seen him, Sherry?'

'You're going to his party, ain't you?'

'*Bill* is your husband?'

'Was.' She turned in an avenue of knotty old magnolia trees.

Professor Graf was not there—a big ground-floor apartment, bare since Sherry had moved out, except for a Confederate flag and some *Playboy* photos nailed to the panelling—but everyone else was: Mr Craig and Mr Kraus, the German philosopher, Power, his wife, Bill . . . .

'C'mon.' Sherry led the way into the bathroom where Chuck—another Graduate Assistant—was pouring a bottle of whisky into the bath. The stopper was in. Mr Dukes—Early Twentieth-Century History—came in with another bottle of Old Tennessee, emptied it in too. I took the cork off my bottle.

'Fuck you and the horse you rode in on—' Mr Dukes put the stopper in the wash hand basin—'That's rye.'

'Went to your lecture on the Spanish American War, Mr Dukes,' I addressed his chest. 'It was great!'

'Thank you kindly. What's your field?'

'You guys going to stand in the john all night?' Sherry scooped a mug of whiskey from the bath.

'Mediaeval sermons.'

'Hard to build huh.' Mr Dukes' eyes followed her out.

'Two plus two equals four.' Mr Craig and Mr Kraus came in, filled their mugs again, stopped to explain how two plus two could as easily equal five. The four of us were pressed up against the radiator. Five, as Bill came in singing: 'Give me that old time religion, that good old-time religion. It was good enough for Pappy, it's good enough for me.'

Radiators everywhere. Probably why Bill was taking off his shirt. His chest was hairier than his head. Inside the dancing had begun. I sat down beside Power and his wife, who had a sort of American accent too. I asked where she was from. From Ireland, I could guess by the way she hated saying.

'The Midlands.'

'County Westmeath,' Power said. 'That right, hon?'

Dympna looked as if she was going to break her mug over his head. 'The Mullingar area. Where are you from?'

'I told you, hon. He was around the corner from me.'

'You were opposite O Braonain, weren't you?' I said.

'How's that guy doing? Heard he was on the funny farm.'

'Let's dance,' Dympna said.

A record player was going now, hard to hear above Bill's singing: 'Let's go git a nigger and r-o-a-s-t him . . . .'

'Nice ass.' Power nodded. Mr Dukes was dancing with Sherry, hands on her bottom. 'Not too big, not too small.'

' . . . And crucify him!' Bill was shouting now, going into the kitchen, coming out with a handful of cocktails sticks, taking off one of his loafers. He pushed Chuck up against the wall. 'What's your thesis, nigger?' Chuck was white, of course.

'Religious Fundamentalism in the Confederate States in the Aftermath of the Civil War'—probably why he knew the Bible so well. As Bill spread out Chuck's arms and began to hammer the cocktail sticks between his fingers with the heel of his shoe, pretending to crucify him, Chuck was able to scream, 'Father, forgive them for they know not what they do!'

'Crucify him!' Everyone else joined in, howling, 'Crucify him!' except Mr Dukes and Sherry, who went out into the magnolia garden.

******

'I cannot help feeling that, with so much material to hand in the "Heath Collection", you should have been able to do more with this topic—.'

Professor Graf's latest comment on my latest paper (again written over some longer comment he had rubbed out) sent me hot and cold to the library to borrow books for next month's paper. He had smiled the Woodrow Wilson smile as he announced it 'The Historiography of Historiography.'

'You wanna lift?'

'Wouldn't say no, Sherry.'

'You wouldn't huh?'

'How'd you get on with Mr Dukes the other night?'

'Getting mighty cheeky, ain't we?' She shoved her sunglasses up as a hairband. 'I just drove him home, same as I'm driving you.'

'Was he drunk?'

'*I* wasn't.'

We drove uphill, turned into Laurel Avenue—each house an old timber palace three and four stories high, four or five undergraduate cars outside. She pointed out hers. 'You come on over for a drink some evening.'

'I will, Sherry.'

I had just dropped my heap of books on the bed when another car arrived. I heard Mrs Storey run to her window. Through mine, I saw Power's Volkswagen. He staggered up the steps with a heap of magazines. Inside my room he raised his chin, let the column topple across my bed. *Playboy*.

'Thought you might be feeling lonely. Three years of it there! Dymps and I got it every month.'

'I couldn't—'

'No sweat. You know,' he lit one of his green cigars and sat on the bed, serious, 'I had a lot of hang-ups. Remember in the Scouts—I was the only one who wore that fucking hat. *I had to* ....' He stood up suddenly. 'But Dymps. Dymps has given me everything.'

'I'll give these back to you.'

'They're yours!' He made for the door. 'Feel like going to the big game with us Saturday?'

'I've all this work—'

'The Vols are playing.'

I pointed to the books, he shrugged: 'Sure, take a raincheck.'

He left his cigar behind. I threw it out the window. Then I put the thirty-six *Playboy* magazines in the chest of drawers and locked it. I put the key in the wardrobe. I locked the wardrobe, put the key under the carpet. I put all the library books on the carpet.

'You OK, Mr Kinney?' Mrs Storey knocked on my door. Her head appeared, snuff juice trickling out of the corners of her mouth.

'Grand! Grand!'

She shuffled down the hall and locked the front door for the night.

******

'Hey, you didn't come see me yet?'

'I'm working every night, Sherry.'

'Where are you going now?'

'Mass.'

'You're one busy boy. What's that?'

'The church.'

'No kidding!'

'We could have lunch together after, if you—'

'Allrighty!'

Father MacGuire was in his flat, which was his vestry too. His mother was laying out his vestments. She left when I said I wanted to make my confession.

208

'Allrighty! Let's hear it.' Father MacGuire put a stole on over his T-shirt and sat down.

I sat down too, confessing the sin of self-abuse.

'Uh-huh.' Father MacGuire looked at his shoes. The laces were still undone. 'A lot?'

'Thirty-six times, father.'

'That's a *lot.*'

'Isn't it, father?'

'You've got to stop. I had to.'

'I'm going to.'

'Allrighty!' He gave me Absolution and tied his shoe laces. His mother came in and helped him with his vestments.

I was so happy, I sang the hymn she played on a harmonium after Communion: 'If You're Going to San Francisco Be Sure to Wear Some Flowers in Your Hair'. There was iced Coke for everyone afterwards in his flat, but I hurried off to Sherry's.

'I thought we were going somewhere?'

'But you can't get booze in a restaurant, not in Knoxville.' She had a bottle of wine opened. In the kitchen there was a saucepan of tinned peas with some red sausages mixed through. 'I'm not much of a cook.' She took off her apron. She had a T-shirt on underneath.

'Nice flat.' I sat down in a corner. There was a plastic hunting-horn on the wall and a print of Gainsborough's 'Blue Boy'. Sherry put on a record—'I Can't Get No Satisfaction'.

'Nice record-player.'

'You like dancing?' She held out her arms.

'Do you?' I whispered and she turned the record-player down—and I heard a car horn blaring outside.

'God damn it, it's Bill.'

I looked out the window. 'No, it isn't. It's Power. Do you know Power, Sherry?'

'Your landlady said you might be here.' Power—long white

shorts and a white T-shirt that said Big Orange—stepped in. 'This is Dick—'

I knew he was Irish before he spoke. He called to a woman behind him, 'Woman, bring in the drink.'

'Telling you about Dick. Married old Kavanagh's sister. Just come down from—wait for it— Alaska! We're all going to see the Vols. Dymps couldn't come. Beverley—'

'Who wants to see the fucking Vols.' Dick pushed past inside. He looked drunk. He looked at me. 'I look familiar? Let's get that shit out of the way. I stole the Goya, got myself photographed outside the gallery, then I handed it back. You saw me in the paper, end of story. Where's the fucking drink?'

'Ssh, love.' Kavanagh's sister came in with an armful of beer cans.

'Hi!' Sherry said.

Dick turned around. He had a high ruddy colour, like someone in from a day's work in the fields. His hair was shining blue black like his eyes. He looked at Sherry from her back-combed streak-blonde hair down to her red-painted toenails. Then he said 'Whore' and turned away into the kitchen. There was a crash as he dropped the beer. Power raised his eyes to heaven as Bill arrived with a strange girl.

'OK. Where's Scott?'

From the noise in the kitchen, Dick was eating up the peas and the sausages. 'Filth.' He came back into the room.

'Who're you?' Bill said.

'I'm a man. Correction. I was a man. I'm a fucking dentist. I look after plastic teeth for plastic people in this arse-hole of a town.'

'Watch your language, boy,' Bill said.

Dick took off his jacket and folded it. It was Connemara tweed. He was wearing a NUI tie. Sherry began to cry.

'Go on—weep!' Dick took a pull at his beer can. 'You can't

210

make beer. You bomb napalm on Vietnam. You fuck up your own country, you fuck up yourselves.' He turned to Bill's girl, flicked the back of his hand across her make-up pitted cheek.

'OK.' Bill took off his glasses. But another door opened and a baby boy, entirely naked, walked in, blinking at the light.

Sherry dried her eyes. 'There's Scott.' She stood looking at him.

'Come on,' Power said. 'We're missing the match.'

'You're right.' Bill put on his glasses and looked at Dick. 'You going back where you came from?'

'Alaska—that's where I came from. I thought I'd find something there, but you've fucked that up too. So I'm here.'

'He's right, you know.' Kavanagh's sister helped him on with his jacket, buttoned the middle button and led him towards the door, stopping each time he stopped.

'—In this fucked-up, fucked-out, arid, barren . . . .'

'Come on, love.'

'. . . Dried-up cunt of a corpse of a country . . . .' His voice rose to a scream.

Scott walked slowly about the room, his eyes blinking less and less as he grew used to the light.

******

'As I read your paper, I wonder whether I should not have insisted on your taking our "English For Foreigners" course.'

No rubbing out this month and Professor Graf had drawn a big easy swirl of a circle around my grade—F.

'I don't think he likes you.'

'I don't think so, Sherry.'

'Give you a lift?'

'I think I'll walk.'

It was winter now. The only one I saw walking these frosty

evenings was Dick, drawing in the air in giant lungfuls, breathing it out as clouds of steam that hung above his head. He was cold sober always now. As I walked alongside, he asked me home for coffee. A lemon-coloured moon sailed in and out through the smog.

'I've been thinking of an island.'

'Why did you come here?'

'Stuck a pin in a map.'

His wife met us at the door. 'Kit's here. He's got toothache again.'

'Let him.'

'He's got a trick with him.'

'Shit!'

'Kit's in the surgery.'

'What's a trick, Dick?'

'Kit's a fag.'

'I see.' I didn't.

Dick swallowed his coffee. 'Show you something while you're waiting.' Through an open door I saw a boy with dyed yellow hair asleep in a black leather chair.

Dick opened another door, switched on a light. 'Won't be a tick. Have a look around.' He shut the door.

It was like a cell somehow: a small room empty except for a full-size Irish tricolour tacked to the wall, a portrait of Sir Roger Casement and a shelf of Irish books. I took down *Twenty Years A-Growing* and sat reading a chapter I remembered—about the teacher who tied Muiris to a post in the classroom, when the priest came in, got angry with the teacher and untied the boys.

The door opened and a fat man, with a face the colour of nicotine, came in. He was panting. He sucked on a dead cigar.

'Where's Kit?'

'In the surgery.'

'OK. I wait here?'

There was a howl, then the boy shouting. 'The tooth! I wanna see the tooth!' And then Dick: 'It's in the bin! The bin!'

'Sure,' I said. 'I'm going actually.'

Actually, I ran. There was a letter for me when I got back to Mrs Storey's. From Father MacNamara. That was a relief.

21

'Em—coffee?' He went to the stove again, one eye shut against the cigarette in the corner of his mouth.

Across the convent park I could see a deer nosing out of surrounding woods. Beyond was Princeton, where we would be going for dinner that evening, he said.

'Sorry I missed you. Last night.'

'I missed you,' he corrected me. 'I forgot.'

He had not come to meet me at the bus station, so I had taken a taxi. He had been asleep when I arrived.

'But I've been expecting you.' He poured black coffee into the white institutional cup set opposite his own on the kitchen table. The priest I remembered from school, sitting at the rostrum table, legs crossed, one toe swinging as he read to us— it seemed an age ago—was gone. Across the table was someone in candy-striped short-sleeved shirt, its pocket filled with glasses, ballpoint and a packet of Lucky Strike. Two lines like brackets on either side of his lips still, and still the the slight lines in his forehead from his habit of holding his eyebrows slightly raised. He looked at his watch. 'Better get the show on the road.' He stood up.

I was a bit put out by his brusquesness until I realised he meant morning Mass. It was St Patrick's Day.

'Brace yourself for a particularly awful em sight.' He opened the door that led from his flat into the chapel, that he had to cross to reach the convent. On the wall behind the altar was a Deposition in cement bas-relief, the bare cross done in chocolate brown. 'My God.' He almost-smiled.

'Good morning, father!' The nuns were wearing shamrock, cascades of it on their habits. They gathered about the vestry to greet their chaplain. 'Happy St Patrick's Day, father!'

The whispery Irish country voices made me wince, but Father MacNamara's brushing past them without a word made me wince even more.

'I've got to go into the university.' Now he was brushing past me, looking for his car keys, gathering up a folder. 'You'd be bored stiff. I'll meet you em same place as last night. The Firestone Library. Five o'clock OK?'

'Firestone at five. OK.'

What to do all day? I wandered around the grounds, which reminded me of school, although at school, there had not been a deer, a wild deer, slipping back into the woods. I went back to the flat and looked through his books—novels and poetry in English and French. One book turned out to be a diary, opening at a page marked with a snapshot of himself, I guessed, as a boy: crombie coat, hair brushed sleek, waving from a train window as if going back to school. I shut it quickly and put it back. I looked into his bedroom; it was in a mess. Of course, I tiptoed in. I opened the wardrobe door. There was such a crash I ran back into the sitting-room. A minute later I tiptoed back and saw a dozen empty whisky bottles rolling about the Turkey carpet. I piled them back into the wardrobe—a black suit swung on a hanger—and shut the door. There were about a hundred cigarette butts in a plate on a bedside locker. The plate was on a copy of *Playboy*. One look at the cover—a girl with a lipstick drawing a bunny on her stomach, her navel its sly eye—and I knew I was lost. Again.

It seemed such a long day. I went back to the diary and opened it where the photo marked a page It was covered in triolets. I read the first line—'I *will* be Bohemian tonight' and then, abruptly as Uncle Paul that day he caught me reading his notebook, I shut it and put it back on the shelf.

Paul . . . Roderick . . . and now Father MacNamara.

'I'll buy this one, then you're on your own.' He sat down at the restaurant table—an expensive one for my first night, a cheap one for the rest of the week. He called the waiter and ordered a Dry Gibson. I had one too. Strong. Ten minutes later, he ordered another, without stopping talking. He seemed to talk all the time. Or at least finished the sentences I began. The talk had returned to Ireland and the Irish priests he knew.

'Father Kiely used to say—' I began.

'I believe he was so dumb, they had to invent a special exam to get him into the Order.'

'Although Father Rowan—'

'I *detested* his particular brand of piety.'

'Of course, Father Wilmot—'

'Of course, all he wants really is to be in the middle of Dublin's middle-class intellectual clique. I suppose that's not too difficult.'

'I thought you got on well together, father?'

'I'd don't think I'd have lasted a week without telling him what I thought of him. Just as well he was out here when I was there. Can't stand that ivory tower crap.'

'Do you not like it here, father?' I caught my reflection—big white smile—in his glass as it paused at his lips. Then—

'Look what the hell did you come here for?'

'Why did you invite me?' I was drunk after one drink.

'As I remember, you invited yourself.' He was not. He turned to catch the waiter's eye. 'Double Dry Gibson, please. You're OK?'

'OK, father.'

'You can cut out the "father" bit.'

'OK.' It seemed as incomplete as Father MacNamara without his gown and Roman collar. 'But you took Father Wilmot's class that year. I mean you took us for Sixth year.'

'If you call putting on intellectual pink tights for the brighter bourgeoisie "taking his class", then I suppose I did.' No pause except to order another drink.

Silence as we drove back to the convent, except for his breath loud in his nostrils.

'Look, I can go if you like.'

'*Stay.*' He started to speak again. 'Not having a car here is like not having legs . . . .' as he stumbled out onto the gravel. He swayed in the dark as he looked up at the stars. They were as bright as in Mayo. '*Les belles etoiles.*' he murmured. But, before I could think of a reply, he was in his bedroom where I heard bottle and glass rattling.

A tapping on the door next morning, a nun's voice whispering, 'Father Andrew . . . a quarter to.'

I tapped on his door. 'Father Andrew . . . .' (by the end of the week it was 'Andrew') '. . . you're wanted.'

'They want their voodoo.' He raised himself on one elbow. '*Sursum corda*' He reached for his cigarettes, '*Habemus* Lucky Strike. Put on the coffee. I'll be back in twenty-five minutes. Sharp.'

'I don't think I'll go, if it's all the same to you.'

'Lucky you.'

I don't think it was just that I had not noticed in the beginning; at any rate, by the end of the week I thought he was looking awful. He didn't shave some days and the stubble covering the fine bracket lines threw out his lips in a strange soft smile. I was feeling better every day. Terrific.

'More rain. The rain—'

'For God's sake, can you not stop *talking!*'

It was true, I thought: we never stopped talking at home. I sat waiting for him to speak. Sometimes he did. 'When I think that, when he was my age, my father had married, was supporting a family, had represented his country abroad . . . .'

'But look at Julius Caesar, Andrew. I mean, what had he done when he was forty?'

Oh, for *Christ's* sake!' He gazed out of the window at the deer. 'Fifteen years. *Fif-teen ye-ars.*'

'What's this, Andrew?'

'Nineteen fifty three I joined. Fifteen years I've been in the Order.'

'Funny—that's the year I went to school.'

He lit a second cigarette by mistake, stubbed it out, drew deep on the first. '*And* school. Mustn't forget old Loyola. Plus six—twenty-one years. Living with it. Holding onto it . . . *WHAT?* '

That was at breakfast. It was usually a bit better at lunch. He had been to see his professor: last details of a doctoral thesis. I had gobbled up another book.

'I was looking at that Hemingway you have, *A Moveable Feast.* '

'There's a nice line in it, isn't there? "All things truly wicked start from an innocence."' He turned to catch the waiter's eye.

'And —' I shoved the conversation along, 'I see you have Douglas Hyde's *Love Songs of Connaught.*'

'"Douggie", as Chas O'Conor used to say.'

'Did you meet Chas?'

'"It is an ancient paederast and he stoppeth one of three", as Ned Burke used to say.'

'About Father O'Conor?'

'I'd say one of these—' he lit another cigarette '—was as far as Chas ever got off the straight and narrow. Em—Dry Gibson, please.'

For dinner, he put on his new tie, a club striped one of crackly polyester, and a check jacket with a collar that was sticking up at the back. They gave his quick weary face a reassuringly gauche look.

'I've written a novel,' I said.

'Yeah?'

'Would you like to read it?'

'What's it about?' He felt for his matches.

'Trying to nail down reality.' I tried to match the offhand voice.

'Forget it.'

'I'll send it to you. If you like.' Because I had finished it, thrown out the manuscript and stood to watch it vanish with the rest of Mrs Storey's bin into the roaring maw of a Knoxville garbage truck. There was just the neat fat folder of typescript on my bedroom table. And I realised that this was the real reason I was here in Princeton—to tell Father MacNamara about it. My home-soaked hero buried, I was ready, eager to step across the gulf to . . . .

'If you like.' He swung his whisky around his glass, gazing through it at me. 'Em—something I often wonder, do college girls still use their virginity as a bargaining counter for marriage?'

'How . . .? Did you . . .?'

'I was around a bit before I joined up. If you could call Law School "around".'

'Why did you join up?'

'Just thought if one—' he smiled at the jargon, 'if *I* was going to make something of my life, I'd better get a move on.'

Silence, deafening as thunder. All I could think of was my hero, Patrick, asleep in a bed of hot rushes in Mayo.

'Dry Gibson, please.' He rested his chin on his hand, gazed about the restaurant. 'See him?' he nodded at a big man with a belly, smoking a cigar. 'He's a millionaire. And he's impotent.'

More silence. He tapped his fingernails on the table. Smiling, he murmured, '*Mensa Mensa Mensam* .' Silence. 'I think if I saw a Latin book now, I'd throw up.'

'Is it true—' I floundered waist-deep through more silence. '—that Father Burke used to bring his bicycle up to his room at night?'

'For a ride?'

'Do you you ever think of going back to Ireland?'

'*Never.*'

'I suppose your family—'

'*Ravening beasts.*'

'Or live in the country, teach in a —'

'I'd rather *die.*'

'I don't know—'

'*Don't.*'

'Still—'

'I said *stay.*'

'I—'

'Then *go!*' He almost-shouted.

The impotent millionaire looked over at us and smiled suddenly through his cigar smoke.

******

The morning I was leaving, he could hardly speak. He sat in the kitchen in a white T-shirt stained with coffee, and blood from a shaving cut, trembling with a hangover. I had never felt better in my life. Never.

'I'll post you my novel when I—'

'Come on, you'll miss your train.' He held onto the table, then onto the door, for a moment onto me—a tiny, electric sensation—as he looked for his car keys. Together we looked in his bedroom, found them on top of *Playboy* on the locker. His bloodshot eye caught mine—'Look, we're not an order of wankers!'

'By the way, Andy' I tried to sound casual.'How do you—'

'Where's my other fucking shoe?'

'Here—but how—?'

'Come on.' He slipped bare white feet into old black shoes. 'Let's go.'

He dropped me at the station, drove away without a word. That only made me feel even more terrific. I bought a paper, got a seat on the train, read the headline. Yuri Gagarin—whom Gorman and I had watched so often curled up in his sputnik as he hurtled high above Rathmines—had been killed in a plane crash .

I had an exciting sense of something at last coming to an end. Slam! Slam! A black porter came down the platform shutting the doors. Then just as the train was pulling out, a man in black leather jumped on, with a girl in black leather too. Two policemen followed, grabbed the man, the girl screamed, the man threw a punch and the police drew their batons. They beat him until he was covered in blood. He seemed to be dressed in shining red leather as they dragged him off the train. Slam!

I was staying the night in Philadelphia with friends of Bill's. Quakers. 'Friends' Bill had called them when he gave me their address. As I was walking down their street, I noticed it was the same one Grandma had worked in . '1167 Walnut,' Aunt Rita had chanted, as if from childhood memory. I passed it on the way—a tall brownstone house, run down and shabby, now turned into a hotel.

'Forever smiling,' Rita had said. 'They didn't understand how someone could be a good worker and happy too.' I pictured Grandma about the same age as myself skipping down those sandstone steps in her maid's uniform. How many times had she walked down this path? Maybe up these steps I was going up now, quite slowly? To deliver a message, say? And asked to stand into this same hall? Maybe even—why not? into this very room.

Bill's Quaker friends' apartment was just one big back drawing room panelled in dark rich wood, with a high ceiling and full-length drapes like stage curtains drawn for the night. The first thing I noticed, though, was a big ricepaper fish hanging from the ceiling, swaying gently from side to side in the current from a gas fire far below, its red-tinted mouth tap-tapping now and then up against the ceiling.

Then as suddenly as I had shut the door behind me, everything in the room began to stir like the paper fish: friends, tables, chairs. There were carved wooden pilasters about my height set along the wooden panels, with small capitals carved into clusters of oak leaves and acorns. Some of the acorn cups had been carved empty and I suddenly looked down at the floor to see if they had fallen there. I was off my head.

It was as if everything had been laid on for a play. Before the drawn curtain was a long table, on it a large book of Aubrey Beardsley drawings, open at a page showing a boy holding a big-as-his-body phallus in his fairy hands.

Bill had phoned they said, was calling for me next morning. Downstairs, they said, lived a prostitute who gave whippings for a living. Sure enough, I thought, when I went down to wash my face with cold water, she appeared on the stairs: very tall, good-looking, with fire red hair down her back and long black leather boots. Upstairs, they said over dinner, was a lesbian commune where they gave pyjama parties. Sure enough, I thought as I lay awake in bed: not a sound. The hot and cold water pipes in the kitchenette had been painted—one fire engine red, the other prussian blue—and they shifted back and forwards before my eyes all night. I dozed at dawn with a cramp in my stomach. When I woke an hour later, I felt dreamily strange.

The young Quaker couple were conscientious objectors to the Vietnam War and were doing alternative service, they told me, as they ground Free South American coffee and heated brown scones for breakfast. Now, I noticed, each like a satyr had a phallus erect.

'What's the position like down south?'

I told them about Maxwell Taylor's rally as I dodged behind the table.

'You heard Bill got his draft papers?'

'I didn't.'

'That's why he's up here. We put him onto a guy who's good on wasting. If Bill can make it down to seven stone, he can get an exemption.'

But Bill must be twelve stone,' I sidestepped quickly.

'It's that or lose a finger.'

Even from the carved empty acorn cups in the capitals, full cocks jutted.

******

Bill talked about his trigger finger all the way back to Tennessee, holding it up as if looking at it for the last time. I looked away as it turned into something else before my eyes. Driving through West Virginia, I looked out at the slate-blue shapes of the Appalachian Mountains. Silhouetted on each ridge, like wayside herms, were a small, a middle-sized, a giant phallus. Bill turned on crackly country and western music. I thought of Father Burke's voice, as he came down our aisle between our desks, holding an illustration from Smith's Classical Dictionary before him, murmuring, 'Some of these fellows seem to have forgotten their mmm goat skins.' But the swelling herms were still there like the KEEP AWAKE signs flashing by.

'Fuck it! I can always light out and change my name.' Bill smiled suddenly. 'Bill Jackson. Let's see. You want something close in case they call your name and you turn. They try that. Jackson . . . Jackson . . . .'

'Who's the guy you're doing for your Ph.D? Johnson?'

'*Johnson!* Goddamn it I'll do it! I'm Bill Johnson!'

'I laughed too, shut my mouth quickly as another cock appeared.

'You got toothache?'

'Nooo.' Sweat ran freely down my back as I risked a wide yawn. 'Sleepy.'

'You hit the scratcher, yo' hear!' Bill shouted after me as I climbed the steps of Mrs Storey's veranda, high as the Appalachians.

'I sure will, Bill!' And I sure did, as soon as I had parcelled and posted off my novel to Father MacNamara, but not to sleep. I did not sleep again for three months until I was back in Ireland.

22

'Well, yourself!'

'Brod! You're home.'

'I am. My father died.' He threw a sack of seed into the back of his van. I got into the front. 'I got married,' he added before I could speak.

'Congratulations.'

He drove up the graveyard hill. From the top, I could see the smoke spiralling up out of his father's circle of lopped trees.

'How're they all above? How's the Dad?'

'Grand.'

'I hear he's after opening a new shop. Where's Stillorgan at all?'

'Outside the city.'

'That's the boy for you!'

'I was in the States myself.'

'I heard that. I heard that. More studying. Are you going on further?'

'I don't know about that.'

'Just for pig iron. And aren't you right.'

I watched his van vanish in blue exhaust smoke up the road. Familiar the bindweed bugles on the hedge, white as the otter's bite in the fish back hill—big as a valley now. Down through it from Galway came a wet July wind, shaking the sycamores, making a noise like the sea. If only—as I got the old scent of meadowsweet and thistles—there was another wall of trees to block out that new bungalow . . . a little ivy over the door . . . and, in some neighbouring lovely lonely old house, some lovely lonely girl. Instead, in the next field now there was a cement-block works and, on the other side—giving off a piercing buzz—

an ESB booster . . . and I was cut off forever from lovely lonely girls because I was . . . my knees went weak with misery as I caught the scent of Margaret's Philadelphus . . . a queer.

'Arra love! Where did you come out of?'

'The three o'clock. . . .' I slipped through her clumsy embrace and she stumbled against the television set, and I said, 'And you got a tv?'

'I did. Oh, you lost weight.'

'How's Austin?'

'He's home. Did they tell you?'

'They did.' I turned on the television and looked at the test card.

'Austin does like it. He must be sheltering. He went down the fields. Are you long back?'

'A week.' I wandered from room to room, calling answers to her questions. Under a heap of *Far East* and *Ireland's Own*, my *Religio Medici* was lying where I had left it ten months before. '. . . United souls are not satisfied with embraces but desire to be truly each other; which being impossible, their desires are infinite and must proceed without a possibility of satisfaction . . . .'

I broke off a crust of bread to rub out my comment in the margin—'Irony breaks through here.'

In ten minutes everything was the same—the new as familiar as the old. The new polystyrene tiles on the bedroom ceilings, the wallpaper patterned with purple antique motor cars, the electric side-lamps: some of them must have been there before I left but I only noticed them now. Austin had retired. Forty years in England and yet, as soon as he sat down to change his wet boots, he too was as familiar as the old scent of dry turf ashes and flour from under the stairs. The tree-creeper was still spiralling

226

out of sight behind the Scots pine, but the wren had gone from the nest in the hinge socket of the big gate—oiled now since Margaret had set the land to the butcher.

Every day the same click of the latch as Austin went down the fields smiling quietly to himself.

'What used you to do on your days off in England?'

'I might walk out the road a bit. Lie in a field. Have a snooze. If it were fine, like.'

If I spoke, he answered. We sat in silence. The fish had gone. The old slaughter-house had turned into a meat-packing factory and red waste water was being let into the river. One of the butcher's bullocks came on us, then another, another gathered round—a circle of dripping snoring noses that drew closer and closer in fascination, scattering as Austin pulled our his pocket watch—'Ooh! time for "Bring Down the Lamp".'

'You like the television?'

'It kills the time.'

Forty years . . . and I had lasted nine months. Austin rubbed a scallion gently in salt. I looked down at my boiled egg, its yolk dark as tea. Above my father's lines of rotting poplars came a cloud of engine smoke, a whoosh! of flames as men burned the day's cement bags. A whoop and a last mad rev of the engine. Then silence.

'Thank God.' I looked up, the cartoonist's white-faced, diamond-eyed intellectual.

'We had silence long enough,' Austin said.

'I never hear them,' Margaret smiled.

'I do,' Austin said. 'I hear them well.'

Margaret turned to me. 'Of course, I can't stand noise myself.'

'If you want to hear noise,' Austin said. 'You will.'

227

'Fancy a jolly old pint then?' Nine o'clock on the dot he was ready, toe-caps and watch chain brilliant in the electric light.

'And do,' Margaret said to me. 'They say a bottle of stout is good for you.'

'Not a bit.' Austin adjusted his cap.

'Well, not a lot now. But the odd one.'

'No good in the wide world, Margaret.' He led the way out and we walked down the warm wet dusty road. From behind the hedges came the coughs of cattle, the crunching of their hooves and the tearing noise as they looped their tongues and pulled juicy tufts of sedge. They went on grazing as a meat container truck shot past, cab windows tattooed with stickers from all over Europe, horn playing the first bars of 'Colonel Bogey'.

'Margaret was telling me about Matt.'

'Ahh!'

'I never thought—'

'He was talking about it long enough. He was talking about it long enough.'

Matt had hanged himself.

Austin was walking very slowly now, stopping at the nearest pub, sitting down heavily on the nearest stool. We had to sit out in the shop anyway, under dangles of boots, buckets and ropes which looked suddenly liked antiques. They were doing up the bar at the back, banging and singing behind a sheet of plywood as if there was going to be a party next day. An electric saw screamed through wood. As if listening to intensely sweet music, Austin rested chin on thumb, a thumb as big as my two thumbs.

The bar filled. He knew everyone; as if he had never left. I tried to join in, but when I raised my voice it sounded namby-pamby superior; when I lowered it, no one could hear me.

'Musha, I don't know what you're saying. Who's this lad, Austin?'

'Eddie's lad.' Austin turned to someone else and left me on my own.

'Now I have you! And how's your Uncle Petie going on? Has he the dropeen on the end of his nose yet?'

'He's never home when I call.'

'Up that green hilleen at the back—that where he does be! I was back there one morning—it wasn't six o'clock—the moon still out and I saw him . . . . Brod! How're you going on?'

Brod nodded and turned to a young woman beside him.

'Vodka and lime.'

'And a pint.' Brod put his hand on her hand, covering her wedding ring with his own: the first married couple I had ever seen in a bar in Ballyhaunis.

'Now, a jolly old sleep.' Austin hummed to himself out of tune as he undressed to his snow white underwear in the dark and slipped into bed. A last Woodbine and then he was snoring softly. At the other end of the room, I lay awake on the new single bed, listening to the rain crackle on the slates overhead, my mind running back yet again to those last terrible months in Tennessee.

'Come on!' Father MacGuire laughed at Communion, waving the handful of creepy campus Catholics in closer with the Host. '—The Lord won't bite!'

He was wrong, I thought. He had hardly left the altar when another terrible thought would clutch me and I had to run after him into the vestry.

'I forgot to tell you, I used to dress up in our maid's clothes.

229

Does that mean I'm—'

'Not here,' he hissed as the black verger looked around. 'Not here.'

The day I went to the campus psychiatrist and afterwards, getting her back turned, managed to read her notes: 'This boy seems intelligent but has got it into his head that he is homosexual.'

Then she thought I wasn't! It was the morning after Martin Luther King's murder. The news had just arrived, as if by Pony Express, in Knoxville and the police were out in force celebrating, cruising through the campus with their elbows on their patrol car horns, echoing my secret elation. *Normal . I* was normal. The beautiful word blared in my head. Normal normal normal.

Dropping my thesis card-index box out of the window, the day I left, another black day, the day Robert Kennedy was murdered. When I stopped off in Princeton, Father MacNamara hardly spoke to me. Open bottle openly on the table now, he was looking at a film of the shooting over and over on his tv. The only time he spoke was when I asked if he had received my novel. He nodded over to his desk, where it lay open, quarter read, and, without taking his eyes off the screen, snapped, 'You'd have been better off going out and getting laid than writing that crap.'

He had driven me to the station. When he dropped me off, he turned his car in a big illegal U. I stood at the station, waiting for him to look back or wave, but even as I waited I knew he would not. He sat slumped down in the seat, so it seemed to be an empty car driving away. I knew that I would never see him again. On the train to New York, I remembered that, accidentally or on purpose, I had left my novel behind.

It was probably still there on that dusty desk, sinking into the peaceful oblivion I had prepared for its hero—and I, I had to be up early in the morning for an interview.

'Go to the ant, thou sluggard; consider her ways and be wise.'

That was the favourite punishment line. There were sheets of it, cancelled by prefects' strokes scattered everywhere. Jotters full of it slipped out of sight as I arrived in class. It was a Protestant school, a small one at that, but it had boys from every county in Ireland. Ireland, but a foreign one to me. Home without home. A decompression chamber as I rose to the surface. You could make out the lonely-looking names—Ludlow, Trowbridge, Faringdon—carved in the soft stones of the roadside walls for miles around, fellow victims of the bends. It was the younger ones, not allowed out on walks by themselves, who tried to run away—Home.

'Sir, you missed it! Poole . . . .'

'Ask Poole his Geography, sir! Thinks Bunclody's in Cavan, sir.'

'Galloping through the whins towards Cavan!'

'Aw, Poole, you big eejit.'

'I'll see you after, Kirk.' Poole turned his pink tear-stained face to me and smiled. 'Mr Morgan fell in the river, sir.'

'Clauber up to his elbows, sir.'

'He caught you all the same, Pooley.'

I sat calmly on a front desk and tried a small yawn. 'Tell me, did I give you memory work?'

'"Ode to Autumn", sir.' Poole smiled up at me from under his long lashes and my knees turned to water. Oh God! Why had he not run in the right direction?

'Poole—"Season of mists and mellow fruitfulness . . . ."'

'Aw, sir! Five minutes.'

Through the big windows I watched the autumn red beech

trees lean before a wind I could not feel. It was warm in here.

As soon as I got my first pay cheque, I had gone to a psychiatrist in Dublin, hesitating at the door—painted bright pink. Say he said I *was* queer? I sat in suspense at the big desk, looking at a picture on the wall—a pair of blue-grey slender hands joined in prayer or repose—while Dr MacPherson went down the first furlong. One's sexuality was not black or white. It related to other facets of the personality. One had, so to speak—he tipped ash from his cigarette into an ashtray the shape of a jewelled butterfly—large *grey* areas . . . .'

I wasn't! I was—oh that nice word again!—*normal*. I managed to make him say it three more times before I paid him.

I was slipping out the pink door into Fitzwilliam Square, pretending to blow my nose into my handkerchief, hiding my face, when I met O'Hara coming in. He was blowing his nose too. I had not seen him for a year. We stood back into the hall and shut the door to talk. He had been coming to El Shrinko, as he called him, for the past six months. So had Spring, Johnson, MacDermot, Fitzgerald and . . . .' O'Hara laughed and rubbed his long bony red fingers together, '*Signor Agnelli.*' I had such a fit of delight I wanted to embrace him—which gave me such a fit of fright I wanted to run back up the stairs to Dr MacPherson. But it was O'Hara's turn now. The secretary was calling his name down the hall. O'Hara—I couldn't understand why he was there—did not even turn around. Cool as ever. 'What did he give you?'

I looked at my prescription. 'Surmontil.'

'Same here. Watch it though. Gives you the runs.' He offered me a Carrolls and began to talk almost seriously. 'I wonder . . . I mean, is *everyone* like this? I mean—' he looked at a woman with knuckles twisted by arthritis slowly shining the brass rail inside the door. '—Is *she* . . . .?'

'Mr O'Hara!' the secretary called loudly.

'Doing anything next Saturday? I'm giving a party. Shrinko's idea. He says I should "meet people".'

'Is there a Mr O' . . . .'

'Coming!' He went up the deep red carpeted stairs.

******

Mr Morgan's eyes followed me around the staff room on Saturday evening. He put another log on the fire and took up a heavy *Life of Sir Thomas Beecham*, as if settling in for the evening. I dawdled towards the door. His upper lip glistened as he smiled. He had had his Antabuse tablet.

'Not going near Mullingar?'

'Dublin, I'm afraid.'

'You could drop me on the way.'

'I'm going another way . . . .' I slipped out the door. The headmaster had made me promise not to give Mr Morgan a lift *anywhere*. I stood a moment to listen. 'I'll have his guts for garters,' Mr Morgan said soberly to himself.

'Did you have your dinner?'

'I'm going down to O'Hara's. He's having a party.'

'Can't you sit down for a minute? This came . . .' As if to hold onto me for another minute, my mother handed me a postcard, Poussin's *The Triumph of Flora* : ' Teaching in a Secondary Mod. Roderick.' Dear Roderick . . . .

'Fleetfoot.' My mother stood at the hall door. Over her shoulder I could see my father sitting in the conservatory, looking out into the back garden. Say, I thought suddenly, I *kissed* her?

I never had. I turned and bumped my lips on her cheek. It went bright pink. She smiled. Through open doors and empty rooms I watched my father get up and walk slowly out the back and stoop, sniff a blossom of the Philadelphus he had slipped from Margaret's one.

'What was it all *for?* he had said, as suddenly and unexpectedly as I had kissed my mother.

'What?' I had blushed. But I knew.

Clang-a-clang! Tranquilla Convent's bell rang. Five to. And now, just as their cypress wall was full-grown, the nuns were leaving, selling their land and going to—of all places—Knock! just down the road from Petie. The world was gone upside down, Mrs Corcoran said. Flats were *the* danger now, Mr Corcoran said.

***

Everyone was at O'Hara's party, all looking at their watches and talking about where they were going on to. Each seemed to be back from somewhere or going away somewhere: Gorman on his way back to Cambridge and more History, Spring out of John of Gods, Fitzgerald out of St Patrick's. O'Hara, who had not only stayed in Dublin but was still living at home, had become as quick as a hedgehog in simple self-protection.

'Must meet for a drink some night.' Corcoran put down his glass at the earliest decent moment.

'That's a date!' O'Hara skipped out of sight into another group. Corcoran tossed a half-pound bunch of keys from hand to hand and stood frowning for a moment before slipping away. On the way to the door, he met someone else and took another glass from the tray Mr O'Hara's old crier was carrying up and down the room. It was as if the house was on fire and everyone kept bumping into everyone else as they made for the exit.

Spring looked terrible, squeezing the palms of his hands about his glass as if in prayer. Johnson's face was grey-white. MacDermot must have been on Surmontil too, I decided, as he slipped off to the toilet again.

'It's like the end of the *Aeneid*,' O'Hara whispered in my ear, then jumped, looking at the open doorway. Through it I saw Father Wilmot take off his coat in the hall. The hall door opened again.

'O'Hara, how *are* you?'

O'Hara jumped again. 'Gin?' He sauntered like greased lightning down the room, leaving me with O'Reilly.

'What are you doing here? I heard you were teaching somewhere in the *bogs*.' O'Reilly flicked open a silver cigarette case. His glassy smile hovered just an inch away from a scowl.

Did I dare—? I had had half a gin and tonic . . . . I raised my spear—his Rothmans—hesitating as Aeneas never had before plunging it into his plump grey flannel thigh.

'Gin-gin!' O'Hara handed him a glass and sped away.

'How's the Law?' O'Reilly almost shouted after him.

'Braw!'

O'Reilly lifted his eyes to heaven, tapped his head with a

235

gold lighter. 'Heard he wasn't too hot up here. What does he expect? Thinks it's for stirring his tea.'

'What do you do?'

'The Bar, actually.'

'I mean, in the line of girls?'

'Look, they piss and shit just like us—' He waved a hand at someone across the the room. 'Look at old Art! You heard he was inside? Breaking and Entering!'

'That's Art?'

'Doing bloody OK now.'

I began to tell him about the time we had broken into our new house together, but O'Reilly got bored. His strange angry-confused face drifted away across the room. I threw his cigarette, my deadly spear, into the fire. It was so hard to draw a bead on those guys. Just as you had them lined up, they said something sensible. Well, it was sensible what O'Reilly said about girls, wasn't it?

'Adrian.'

I turned, saw Mary Cole. Oh no it wasn't, never would be, not while she stood shoes together like that. She drew back an invisible strand of hair.

'I was talking about you the other day,' she smiled. 'I met your cousin—John, who was in the army.'

'How is he?'

'He's getting married, he said. She keeps horses, he said.'

Someone tall and thin appeared at her side, slipped his arm through hers and she said, 'I'm getting married too. You never met Tim?'

He nibbled the ends of a mousey moustache and Mary Cole's smile faded. As he led her away, Gorman appeared beside me, blowing tonic bubbles from his new beard.

'He's in advertising. She met him that summer we were in Greece.' Gorman stroked his beard, smothering a small yawn,

236

another. It was an amazing beard. His face had disappeared behind it. But, when he talked about Cambridge and History, about the latest politics—Northern Ireland was the place to watch now—he talked just as he used to talk about Suez, Nasser and King Hussein.

'Any news of O Braonain?'

'You didn't hear? He's working for your father.'

I tried to imagine O Braonain on his knees, selling shoes. To my surprise, I could—easily.

Across the hall in the library cum living-room, three shelves of books and the green-nosed caricature of de Valera were gone, hidden by a television set.

Mrs O'Hara caught my glance. 'How the mighty are fallen!'

Mr O'Hara smiled, looked back quickly at the tv. Even with Father Wilmot there, he had the set turned on, gazing fascinated at some travel film.

'You're back.' Father Wilmot shook hands. He was in lay clothes, yet they made him seem more like a priest than ever.

'How's Father MacNamara?' I blurted, skipping small talk, as if rushing to the last page of a novel.

'Laicised, I believe. I think he might be happier now.' He made a calm gesture, as if summing up the Latin Mass, maids, floggings and charcoal suits. 'You came at the end of that world.'

'I've been hearing that all my life.' Mrs O'Hara stubbed out a cigarette. 'And it's still the same world.'

'Similar.' Father Wilmot made a qualifying gesture and turned back to me. 'And you're teaching now? Do you like it?'

'No.'

'And what . . . ?'

'I don't know.'

He made another gesture of graceful calm, as if playing an invisible piano chord.

O'Hara appeared in the door. 'What's on the box?' He

peered with longing at the tv. Some bronzed man in flapping white shirt was down on one knee, pointing at what seemed like a prehistoric creature's footprint in parched cracked mud.

'Jim . . . really.' Mr O'Hara glanced over his shoulder.

'I've got to go.' I got to my feet.

'Is it . . . far?' Voice uneasily vague as it was when speaking of the country, O'Hara walked me to the door.

I thought of that crossroads signpost—Dublin 60—still lying against the broken ditch and realised that the job I had landed in, so haphazardly, was exactly halfway between my two homes. That was why I was there. I had no home now. 'I' . . . 'I'—the word seemed as ghostly unreal as the moths fluttering about the streetlamps, as beautiful too.

'No,' I smiled. The door swung shut.

I began my drive in the dark.